MEDIC ONE
ON SCENE

MEDIC ONE
ON SCENE

Dr Heather Clark

First published in Great Britain in 2001 by

Virgin Publishing Ltd
Thames Wharf Studios
Rainville Road
London W6 9HA

ISBN 1 85227 883 9

Typeset by TW Typesetting, Plymouth, Devon
Printed and bound by Mackays of Chatham,
Lordswood, Kent

To Stephen Niland
hoping that he will continue to be as lucky
for the rest of his life

Author's Note

To protect patient confidentiality the details surrounding some of the incidents described in this book have been fictionalised. Medical treatments and emotions are all based on personal experience.

Contents

Acknowledgements

I would like to express my thanks to Helen Armitage and Jeff Gulvin for their help in writing this book.

A special thank you also to Mark whose help and support kept me going through the difficult patches.

MEDIC ONE
ON SCENE

1 One Under

THE PLASTIC SHEET HAD BEEN ERECTED on the platform so that no one could see what was going on, but in reality it's hard to keep prying eyes away. Behind that crude blue curtain we fought to save a man's life amid an incongruous mix of blood and flying feathers. He had tried to kill himself by leaping under a train and every time one rushed by we were engulfed in a whirlwind of feathers, fluttering around from what was left of his down-filled jacket. Like snowflakes they descended on us, making it hard to see and harder still to work. The feathers stuck to us like glue, there was blood on our hands, arms and uniforms. It was everywhere. I was covered in it and, with the white feathers and red blood and my bright-orange flying suit beneath, I must have resembled a half-plucked chicken. Farcical to look upon and yet there I was battling to save someone's life, someone who themselves had decided it wasn't worth living.

We were on line from 7.30 a.m. to sunset, 365 days of the year. For six months this was my life, a flying doctor with the Helicopter Emergency Medical Service (HEMS). There were no days off. Every one of us loved the job so much we would volunteer to do weekends. It is the only medical job I've known where this happens. 'Medic One' is the first team on call; whenever a spare day came up we would fight over it, which team got it often decided on the toss of a coin.

Even now, though officially I have left, I still work voluntarily with HEMS to keep my hand in, and because I miss it. I miss everything: managing trauma, the people, the teamwork, the fact that you're really helping. Work like that gets under your skin, not so much a job as a way of life. A career in medicine would probably be deemed vocational anyway, but this really is the sharp end. It's exciting, and you save lives. It is work where you actually know you save lives. It is very dramatic, very tense, but I operate well under those conditions. I am calm – very calm and quiet. Some of the doctors can be a bit frenetic. Others shout orders: Do this! Do that! Get this done now! Slightly panicky maybe, or just the adrenaline pumping. I tend to be fairly quiet – I ask rather than order. Do you mind doing this? Thank you.

Different people handle things in different ways, situations, crises, opportunities.

I thought I was different. I thought I could do this job and walk away. I thought it wouldn't get to me like it would someone who was medically untrained. But I was wrong.

In October 1999 I was travelling on the underground system on my way to start an MSc in Sports Medicine. I had left HEMS in the September and taken a short watersports holiday in Greece; I was back, fresh and ready to begin again. It was my very first day, and I was *en route* to college for my inaugural lecture. As I got on to the platform I recognised where I was immediately: this was the tube station where some months earlier I had tried to resuscitate the man who had jumped under a train.

Spring: my first day with HEMS and my first case. A 999 call had come in to the HEMS desk at Central Ambulance Control (CAC) in Waterloo. It was an Immediate Dispatch, which usually meant we were at the patient's side within ten minutes. The siren, triggered by the CAC's call, rang at the HEMS base on the sixth floor of the Royal London Hospital in Whitechapel. It's unlike any other siren, a warning alarm that invades your senses, demanding immediate action. I never got used to it. It rang every day for six months and I never got used to it. From the moment it was triggered we had three minutes to scramble.

That afternoon we went by car, the incident being close enough to the hospital to make the helicopter unnecessary. Laurence was with me – a doctor who had been with HEMS for several months, and whose job that day was to give me some specialist training. For the first month every doctor is paired with someone more experienced until you have learned the ropes and your confidence is up.

A 'One Under' is HEMS shorthand for a suicide leap in front of a train. When we arrived on scene the patient was lying on the platform, having been thrown back by the force of the impact. He was conscious but deteriorating fast. We began to work immediately, according to the very strict protocols that prevail. We stabilised the head and neck then secured the airway. We started taking off his clothes to make a full assessment. We have to have full access to the body. His life was slipping away from him, and the team worked frantically, in unison, people on all sides. I started cutting off his clothes, down each side, arms, legs. The whole top layer comes off and afterwards you are left with an imprint on the ground. It is a system that makes it easy for us to work.

The patient was wearing a down-filled padded jacket, and as I cut through it the feathers started to fly, the wind blowing like a gale through the underground tunnels every time a train passed through. It is preferable not to stop the trains during an incident like this because their ventilation relies on movement. If the trains are stopped for long periods you could end up with a major emergency due to lack of oxygen and overheating. We keep them running, but they don't stop at the subject station – they fly straight past and no one is allowed to get off.

Day 1 of my six-month stint with HEMS: a gory and grim introduction. When it was over the patient was dead and I emerged into the light and warmth of a spring afternoon covered in blood and feathers. The patient had not stood much of a chance. He must have wanted to die very badly. Six months later as I took the escalator above ground I could hardly believe I was the same person who had been at the scene that day. The memory disturbed me, acute all at once, deep and painful. Yet the previous spring I had felt nothing. Of course it was horrific and awful, but at the time the patient is simply another unfortunate casualty and, however heartless and uncaring that might sound, that's how you cope with the job. Half a year later, however, I was a commuter – I was no longer there in any medical capacity and I was gripped by a terrible sense of sadness.

Another bright morning but October now and I made my way towards college, the image of that dying man and our desperate attempts to save him in my head. Maybe it was my mood, maybe just coincidence, but I had not gone far when I came to a big road junction and realised it was the scene of one of my very last cases. Strange how events can conspire against you, the first and last almost in the same breath. There on the railings was a photograph of a patient who had died. It was ringed by bunches and bunches of flowers. I stood for a long moment and stared at the silent memorial, a slow sense of desolation threading the path of my veins. And yet the rational still edged this sudden emotion and I thought how bizarre it was that all this was affecting me today, when at the time I had simply signed the form, Pronounced Life Extinct.

The proximity was closer: September. A pedestrian had tried to cross the road at the same time as an articulated lorry was taking a left-hand corner, and when I got to the body, it was unrecognisable.

The helicopter was already out when we received the call. I was Medic Two that day, second on call. They asked the usual: 'Can you respond?'

We were ready to go. We were always ready to go and just grabbed our gear and hurtled down the road. It was pouring with rain, and there was already a crew on scene who immediately told me it was a 'purple plus'. That's unrecoverable. 'Purple' and 'purple plus', are ambulance terms that mean dead and unrecoverable. These paramedics hadn't even attempted resuscitation. The injuries were so severe they knew it was pointless. As the doctor on scene I still had to check whether the victim was alive or dead. Tragically, the victim was dead.

The driver of the articulated lorry could not even have seen the pedestrian on his inside line, close to the kerb. The patient's injuries were some of the most horrific I've ever seen – the skull and head crushed flat. Thinking back as I stared at the railings that day, it was an awful sight, yet at the time I simply checked the pupils, tested the pulse, watched to see if there were any signs of breathing. One, two, three, four – ten seconds. That's all it took then I just signed the PLE sheet, standing beside the body with rain plastering the tarmac. The paper was soggy and the ink ran as I tried to write notes.

I gave up and went to speak to the lorry driver. He was sitting in a police car, pale, drawn, the kind of pallor to his skin that only extreme shock can give. He told me he had a flask of tea in the cabin of his lorry, so I clambered up to get it for him. I sat there for a few moments and it was all so clear. High up in the cab, looking down on the world with near vision impossible, how could he have seen the man? He couldn't have. I imagined how the pedestrian had tried to make a dash across the road, in a hurry to get where they were going, out of the driving rain.

This was as much thought as I gave it, just the details, the practicalities of an accident. I signed the PLE, and went on to the next job. But that October afternoon I arrived at college for the start of my Sports Medicine course feeling very different. As a doctor I had witnessed many grisly sights – that goes with the territory. Most of the time it's just the job, what you do, what you were trained for. It didn't normally affect me. But take it or you out of the professional context and it becomes human. You become human. I sat down for the first lecture absolutely gutted.

I could not get it out of my mind, once I was susceptible to the thoughts, the memories, it came at me from all sides. I sat through the first day's lectures and remembered how the rest of that ferociously wet day had unfolded, how we'd gone from one horrific accident to another. While still on scene with the dead pedestrian we received a call to a fire-related incident in a bedsit. Back in the car we raced through the driving rain, barely able to see through the windscreen, wipers flicking back and forth like a whiplash. We arrived to find an old man burned beyond belief. I can only assume he had been smoking in his bed. Whatever he had been doing he'd set fire to himself. He lay there charred and black and smoking.

I shall never understand how nobody smelled the smoke. The scene was one of utter devastation. How could a fire get that bad that quickly? Somebody must have smelled something. But apparently they didn't, and the fire took hold. It was contained in the one room, the bed even, just the old man and his bed, as if he had spontaneously combusted. When I got to him he was still conscious and talked with lucidity to me. His bed was black, soot-like, a cinder from top to bottom. He was no longer in it: somebody had got him out, but not before the bed had burned completely.

He was going to die. I knew it, and I think he knew it. I knew by the percentage of burns: at first glance they looked in the region of 90 per cent. Severe burns are terrible to deal with. Despite the severity of the injuries and the inevitable outcome, the patient can talk to you and make sense. This old man was talking to me, lying there, black, his legs burned through to the bone, his eyes wide and open looking at me.

I knew I had to anaesthetise him – had to protect his airway. If I didn't he could not be moved: he would be in so much pain, his nerve endings frayed and exposed all over his body. He was already in agony, and still he could talk: 'Please. Let me speak to my wife before I die.' I knew that if I put him to sleep, he would probably never recover. The ventilator would be switched off and he would never wake up again; he would never speak to his wife. What was I to do – leave him in agony so he could have one last word with his wife? Or put him to sleep, humanely, quietly, and take the pain away? It was an impossible decision, but if I was to save him, he needed oxygen and, with a burned airway, I needed him to be asleep to achieve this. I injected him with an anaesthetic, and as I did I comforted myself with the knowledge that even if his wife had managed to get to his bedside, he wouldn't have been in any fit state to see her. He probably wouldn't have recognised her, and I am sure that the situation would have been deeply distressing for her.

After I had administered the anaesthetic, I intubated him – that is I put a tube down his airway to help him breathe. As I did so I saw deep down into his lungs, and visualised soot between the vocal chords. This, combined with severe inhalation burns, was another bad sign. We covered the body in dressings, as usual wrapping the burns in clingfilm. This stops the air getting to them and makes them less painful.

We took him to hospital because, although we knew there was no hope for him, he had to go somewhere. By the time we got him there and into the resuscitation room he was unrecognisable. But he was spared any further pain and indignity when shortly after admission, mercifully, he died.

The smell of a human body burning is one of the worst smells you will ever experience, and it lingers. You can not get it out of your nose afterwards. It didn't leave me for the rest of the day. In hindsight I would say that this was one of my worst days, but I coped. I had to. I could not have done the job if I had not got the stomach for it.

2 Stepping Out

I GO INTO THINGS HEAD on. I always have done and I'm sure I always will. It can be a nightmare for my friends and probably for my family, although I suppose they're more used to it having known me longer. I have always got to have something happening, and usually have a million things on the go at once. But there was one thing that I knew I wanted to do from when I was very young, and that was to dance. By the time I was two and a half I was hooked: dancing became the passion that has consumed me ever since.

It started at the local Westbury School of Dancing, where my mother took Julie, my older sister, to help build her confidence. Julie was very shy as a child. I sat on my mother's lap at the back of that first class and refused to sit still. I was so excited by it all and, even though I was barely old enough to walk, I was enrolled the following week. I learned all the dance steps along with the rest of the students, and I have been dancing ever since. When I was just three I was taken to see Margot Fonteyn perform at the Bristol Hippodrome. My family tells me that at the point in the performance when Fonteyn's partner lifted her high in the air, I announced in a loud voice: 'I want a man to pick me up like that!'

I never looked back. I have been a ballet fanatic all my life and its appeal has never diminished. My first stage appearance was at the Bristol Eisteddfod at the age of three to perform a duet with the four-year-old daughter of my dance teacher. We were both tiny, and the choreographer had coached us to enter from opposite wings, stage left and right. I made my entrance only to find myself alone on stage – my partner had got stage fright! Pretending I had a partner anyway, I danced on. I seemed to know it intuitively, even then, that no matter what happens the show must go on.

The whole of my childhood and adolescence was absorbed by dance. I was constantly performing in ballets or doing shows, often with the Bristol Light Opera Company. My most memorable appearances were as one of the princesses in the *King and I*, when I was seven, and subsequently as Louisa, one of the von Trapp children in *The Sound of Music* – both at the Bristol Hippodrome. I lived and breathed dancing and acting. By the time I was ten I had a regular dance partner, Adam James. We were of similar age and stature, and a winning combination from the moment we started together in the Bristol Eisteddfod.

Adam and I were entrants in a dance competition at the Victoria Rooms in Bristol: I was 12 or 13, just beginning to develop with puberty coming on. We were on stage in the middle of our performance when Adam lifted me in a particularly tricky movement. I heard an ominous ping, and when next I raised my arms my dress didn't come with them. The bodice had split, and I was in danger of appearing topless on stage. Through his smile Adam hissed at me, daring me to let go of my dress. I refused. There are limits, even I know that, though most of my life I've hated to be constrained by them.

None of this hampered Adam's career as a dancer. In his mid-teens he won a place with the Royal Ballet, the first black dancer ever to do so, and later joined the Harlem Dance Company in New York. I did not lack opportunities either. Not long after the bodice-ripping incident I was spotted by one of my dance teacher's former pupils, then a principal dancer with the Royal Ballet Company. Sitting in on a class, he was sufficiently impressed to arrange an audition for me backstage at the Hippodrome with Gerd Larsen, the then ballet mistress of the Royal Ballet. Based on that audition I was offered a place at the Royal Ballet School. I was ecstatic until they told me the place was conditional. Ballet dancers tend to be a specific size and shape and, after taking my bone measurements, it seemed unlikely I would reach more than five foot one in height and might become a bit too curvy. It was therefore possible that after a year with the Royal Ballet School I would have to leave.

It was the mid-70s, and Wayne Sleep was a rising star in the firmament of the Royal Ballet at the time. They were looking for someone to partner him, and it could have been me! Wayne Sleep is tiny and, if I had proved outstanding, then the lack of height might not have been such a problem. But that was jumping way into the future and, as it has a tendency to do, real life intervened.

I had just left my primary school, Amberley House, where in my final year I had been head girl, and started at Red Maids High School on a scholarship. If my year at the Royal Ballet school did not work out, there would have been no free place to return to, and no possibility of my parents being able to afford any school fees. I stood to lose out all round, so efforts were made to convince me that because the place at the ballet school was conditional, none of this was sensible. Reluctantly I agreed. Although it took a lot of time, eventually, tearfully, I reconciled myself to having lost the chance of a career in ballet. It was a devastating thing to accept, as ballet had been my entire life from as far back as I could remember. Even now I sometimes wonder what may have happened if we had all just bitten the bullet and gone for broke that year.

I continued to dance for fun, however, because it was in my blood. I still did shows with the Bristol Light Opera Company. I was quite committed to it, and although I knew it was not going anywhere I even cut off my hair when I was 16 for an appearance one Christmas as Peter Pan. I had always worn my hair long but for that show I let them crop it into a short bubble top. I hated the way I looked, but I tend to go into everything I do wholeheartedly, and there was no way I would have chickened out. This was a production in which I had to fly – they put me on a wire and I soared above the stage. It was thrilling and, come to think of it, good preparation for HEMS, well at least after a fashion. I have never been afraid of heights or had any fear of flying!

I tried to apply myself with the same enthusiasm at school, where I had never done any real work other than that involving drama. I did some Shakespeare: as Ariel in *The Tempest* and Shylock's maid in *The Merchant of Venice*, and played Grimalkin (the cat) in *Bug Eyed Loonery* by Brian Bishop. When it came to academic studies I had always done the absolute minimum. I have a good short-term memory, which generally meant I could sail through exams with the minimum of effort after revising at the last minute. I got 13 O Levels with very little fuss, but when it came to choosing A Levels I was lost. I only wanted to be a dancer; there was nothing else. But I had to face reality, so I opted for Chemistry, Biology and Maths with Physics and Statistics A/O Level. When it eventually came time to decide on a career choice, I took what I then saw as the line of least resistance.

I had never experienced a burning desire to be a doctor, nothing like I felt with dance. Basically I fell into medicine by chance. I actually wanted to be a vet, but knew my A-level grades would not be good enough. I therefore decided I would go into nursing, but everyone told me that I was too clever, and should become a doctor instead. I secured provisional places at medical school at both Birmingham and St Mary's in London, but when I got my A-Level results I had not achieved the grades required for either of them. When St Mary's said they would take me anyway I remained relatively unmoved. Some people, probably most people who enter the medical profession, do so because it is their life's ambition, their vocation. That certainly wasn't true for me.

I was 18 and really naive when I first left home. I suppose I had led a pretty sheltered existence, and my experience of the opposite sex was minimal. I had been a day-girl at Red Maids, an all girls boarding school. I had no brothers. I had never been someone who went out with friends from school to the cinema or clubs and suchlike. I used to go to ballet classes and rehearsals and then spend my free time at home stretching my legs and practising my steps.

I arrived in London in autumn 1982 to study medicine at St Mary's and found myself in the middle of Paddington's red-light district. All I could see from the window of my room overlooking Praed Street was a parade of prostitutes. I was horrified. As it turned out life in a medical school was not any easier for me to fit into either. I had nothing against alcohol, but I did not drink – I just did not like it. Even now I am a minimal drinker, the odd glass of wine, and that's it. But medical school equals drinking. It is a beer-swilling culture, and not joining in with that meant that I was inevitably a bit of an outsider. I was also out of step with the other students when it came to my wardrobe. While they mostly wore the undergraduate uniform of jeans and a T-shirt, I wore a sensible blouse and corduroy skirt that I had made myself. I shall never forget that skirt: when I looked at it a year later I finally realised just how twee it actually was. After a year in medical school I cringed with embarrassment that I could ever have thought it wearable.

Changing on the outside was easy, the surface alterations required to adapt to a given situation. Inside, however, I remained something of the wide-eyed innocent. This was not helped by my choice of boyfriend, who I discovered early on to be very possessive. He was my first real romance: slightly older, in the year above me and from a Greek Cypriot family that still lived in Cyprus. He was clear from the start that he would prefer me not to mix with the other students, and during my first two and a half years of college I made few friends apart from him. Neither did I join anything, no clubs, no drama societies, no dancing classes – in fact, for that two-and-a-half-year period I did no dancing at all.

It was as if I had consciously closed the door on that side of my life. I was preoccupied with anatomy, biochemistry and physiology, and I had my first taste of dissection, and of the smell of it – the pungent stench, predominantly formalin, a disinfectant and preservative used in biology labs. It hit me as soon as I walked into the huge dissecting room.

I shall never forget the rows of dead bodies, shapeless mounds beneath white plastic sheets. There really is nothing as lifeless as a dead person: when the sheets were pulled back, they just lay there like lumps of yellowed meat. I had no idea that that happened when people died – that the flesh loses its natural colour, and turns a mucky jaundiced yellow. It was hard to believe that anyone had ever been alive in such hollow, empty husks.

There were 100 or so other students in my year, and separated into groups of six we were each allocated a cadaver. We gave names to them – mine was called Harriet. She was invaluable to me and I got to know her well, because I worked on her for the best part of a year. If anyone ever tells you dissection is easy, do not believe them – it is not. Sometimes you just cannot find things, the right organ or whatever. Other times you find things you are not expecting at all, such as Harriet's false teeth popping out of the aperture when we opened up her neck.

Dissection involved no loss of dignity for Harriet, but loss of my own dignity was very much what I feared the day I spotted male anatomy on the timetable. I was horrified at the prospect of having to say out loud any of the names of the parts of the male anatomy in front of my peers. I was far too shy even to contemplate it, mortified at the very thought. I skipped that class, which at the time was no great loss because I was not working too hard anyway. When it got to the summer and examination time, however, I realised I was going to struggle. I did what I could, but there were a lot gaps – apart from the male anatomy, I hadn't even got round to the leg. This got me into trouble in the orals, and how I managed to scrape through I shall never know.

Part of the problem was that I had got through school so easily. When it came to medical school I found myself with a more select group of people, and suddenly I had to work. I was not used to it, not used to it at all. But the heart of the matter lay in the fact that I didn't want to be there in the first place. I had vowed that if I failed the exams that first year I would not go back. But I was too proud to fail. Right throughout my time at medical school, each year I would say, I'll just do this year, and then I'll leave at the end of it.

There were compensations and distractions of course; one of which was Rag Week. I did the usual range of silly things from hijacking a double-decker bus to playing Dying Ants and lying down in the middle of the Marble Arch intersection with hundreds of other white-coated would-be doctors. This was great fun but did nothing to curb my reservations about what I was doing there, and certainly not enough to stop me from feeling homesick. Every time I went back to Bristol I didn't want to return to London. My mother used to have to almost shove me bodily back on the train, muttering encouragement in my wake. I wasn't desperately unhappy, but I would not say that my years at university were the best of my life, which is what a lot of people say. For me, those tutelage years were there to be got through and that was about it.

During that first summer vacation I went back to Bristol to live with my family: my mother Mavis, and my stepfather Bev. I am very close to my mother. I think we are quite alike and my never-ending energy probably comes from her. She left school at 16, was married at 21, and always regretted not having gone to university. Not so long ago she took herself off to college to study art and has recently qualified with a BA.

She paints the most magnificent watercolours. She is very artistic but, unlike me, she prefers to be in the background, doing the costumes and set design. Like me, she enjoys the theatre, though she would never go on stage herself.

My parents separated when I was five. She and my father, Ken, had married young, and stayed together until their mid-twenties. I do not remember a specific reason for their divorce, and the most they will ever say now is that they were not compatible. I didn't like Bev when we were first introduc-ed, hardly surprising when I saw him as a stranger who was trying to take the place of my father. Now he is one of my best friends and I realise that it must have been tough for him to take on two young children.

I wish I saw more of my father but work and circumstan-ces make it difficult. When he was younger he was a competitive sportsman, playing tennis, table tennis and squash at high levels. I get my sporty and competitive streak from him. These days he has slowed down a lot. In fact he has just retired from Clark's Pies, the family business where I used to work when I was still at school, doing the pastry twirls that go on the top of Cornish pasties and cutting up the kidneys for the steak and kidney pies. All the pies are freshly made and locally celebrated, sold either direct or through fish and chip shops and pubs in Bristol and Wales.

The company has its origins in Cardiff where, during the depression, my widowed Welsh great-grandmother and her seven children were rescued by a Salvation Army officer from a doorway where they were found sheltering, penniless and homeless. They were accommodated in the church hall; their living quarters at one end of it screened off every Saturday night for dancing. Here my great-grandmother redeemed herself by virtue of being a good cook. Pies were her speciality and she made extra batches for the neighbours. Eventually she began to not give them away but sell them, and Clark's Pies became a thriving concern. A few years later she came across the same Salvation Army officer who was down on his luck. In repayment for his earlier kindness she taught him to make pies and set him up with a business in Bristol. On his retirement he handed it back to the family and my grandfather and his brothers took over from there.

That first summer back in Bristol I earned my keep with a succession of holiday jobs. Waitressing, I liked immensely; it is a very social job, and I always enjoyed chatting with the customers. I like people, and as a doctor I have always liked patients, that is a part of doctoring that I particularly appreciate. I worked as a cleaner at St Mary's, a private hospital in Bristol, which was a bit of an eye opener. When the patients thought I was merely a cleaner, it was a case of 'Do This', 'Do That', 'Change the Water in My Flowers', with not so much as a please or thank you. But when word got round that I was a medical student they all wanted my advice on their hospital treatment.

I took a job in a greengrocer's shop that involved a lot of lifting, mostly sacks of potatoes. I am reasonably strong, so that helped, and I am vegetarian, so it was more appropriate than chopping up kidneys at Clark's Pies. It is not that I am a morally minded vegetarian, it's just that I do not like the idea of eating animals. I still enjoy pepperoni on my pizza though!

Equally, I am not a great drinker. I was not put off pulling pints round the corner from where I lived in London. The Truscott Arms in Shirland Road sells ten real ales – it was famous for them. There was something known as the 'Truscott challenge', which involved drinking all ten different beers in the one evening. If you were still standing after that, your name was chalked up on a board. I worked as a barmaid one or two nights a week for a number of years, and loved it. Like being a waitress, it is very sociable and we had a lot of regulars so I got to know a wide range of people. When someone wanted to buy me a drink the landlord let me put 50p in a cup to bolster my wages. That was useful because, living on a grant, you are always short of cash. The only real drawback was the way my clothes and hair reeked of beer and cigarette smoke when I got home.

During term time I also worked at the Wellington, a big private hospital in wealthy and fashionable St John's Wood. I was a phlebotomist, a blood taker, and the main reason I worked there, apart from the money (which was good) and the Danish pastries (which were even better) was the fact that I was able to study between patients.

I was at the end of my second year and still involved with my Cypriot boyfriend. He'd gone back to Cyprus for the summer, and I decided to surprise him by getting myself a job there and joining him. I had other Cypriot friends in my year, and they helped me to arrange it. When I phoned him once I had arrived in Limassol, and told him excitedly that I was there in Cyprus, he was the one who surprised me. Quite matter of factly he announced that he could not see me. His parents would not allow it. I was the wrong religion, the wrong social class – the wrong wealth bracket for their son.

I was stunned. We had been together for two years. I couldn't believe he would not stand up to his parents for me. But he told me he felt indebted to them because they were paying his fees to study medicine – how could he walk away from that?

I saw him twice that summer. The rest of the time I did a nightmare stint as a nanny, with minimal time off. The child was blond, his parents Greek, with olive skin and jet-black hair. The wife, an anorexic, had had major problems conceiving, and when their son was born, whole and healthy and with fair hair, they treated him as if he were a little changeling prince. He behaved like a spoilt brat but they refused to discipline him.

I was more than pleased to return to England in the autumn, leaving the nannying and the boyfriend well and truly behind me. Although we both returned to St Mary's that October, our relationship was over. It had been built on false promises and lack of fundamental respect. The only good that had come out of my trip to Cyprus was my having learned to water ski. Of course, being me I didn't just learn to ski. I threw myself into the sport so passionately that I even take to the English waters in December.

I know I am someone who develops passions in life: I go into something with every ounce of energy and commitment I can summon. Yet, I still didn't feel that way about studying medicine. Consequently, instead of returning to medical school to start year three, I took time away to do a BSc in Chemical Pathology and Clinical Pharmacology. Only the top ten students from each year who apply are selected, and I was lucky enough, or good enough, to be one of them. I had worked hard in my second year, much harder than my first, having learned that I could no longer rely on short-term memory to get me by. I had done well by the end of it, even though I had contracted a bad case of chicken pox just before my exams.

I had been ordered home, and my stepfather came up to London to drive me back to Bristol and look after me for the week. I felt desperate. Given my ambivalence about becoming a doctor, I seriously wanted to do the BSc. I had got sick the week before the exams, which was of course the week in which I normally do all my cramming. I spoke to my tutor, telling him how ill I was and that I could not study, that I was not going to pass. He reassured me that it was the work we had done during the year that mattered, and that being out of the running the week before wouldn't make any difference. Naturally, I knew otherwise. I knew I never retained anything unless I read it the night before. I was famous for it. One of the reasons I had passed my first-year exams by the skin of my teeth was because I had not slept for a week. I had stayed up every single night. I couldn't do it now, but at that age I was young enough to manage. I studied 24 hours a day, and finding it more distracting to work by day, I did my most effective study at night.

This time I felt passing or failing was more a matter of life and death. Although I had no particular plans about where the BSc would lead me, it would open things up beyond medicine: another academic degree made more career possibilities available to me. I felt it would broaden my horizons, and I wanted that more than anything.

3 Kinango Without a Map

I 'VE ALWAYS THOUGHT THAT LIFE is like dance: you spend your time learning the steps. That's certainly how I viewed my life – sometimes I stumbled and got the steps wrong, other times I did not falter at all, my feet barely touching the ground. That was how I had felt the day I heard I had a place on the BSc course. I was dancing flawlessly, steps learned and executed to perfection. I didn't know where I was going, what avenues would be opening up before me, but there would be choices, decisions to make and the excitement of discovery thrilled me.

I did the degree at St Mary's and Hammersmith hospitals, and wrote my research thesis on 'The role of calcium in the dopaminergic inhibition of prolactin secretion in rat anterior pituitary'. Now there's a mouthful if ever I uttered one. When it was over I returned to St Mary's, and in the autumn of 1985 I started my third year as a medical student. By now I had a new boyfriend, Robin. We had met when I started dancing again, in a show staged by the medical school. I had begun to join in fully, getting involved in things that I loved – acting and dancing in college productions. Things got much better after that and Robin was no small part of it. I was enjoying a fresh start in more ways than one: I'd become more sociable and made new friends – Ann for example, with whom I've remained in touch.

Ann and I shared a number of dreary student flats, truly grim accommodation. We frequently moved on, literally wheeling our worldly belongings through the streets of west London on a luggage trolley borrowed from Paddington Station like two old bag ladies or an evicted family from a Dickens novel. Looking back I can't quite believe some of the dumps I rented, living with all sorts of people, one of whom turned out to be a kleptomaniac, stealing her way through life. For months I wondered if the washing machine was eating my clothes. Things would go missing here and there, more than the one sock that habitually haunts the drum of washing machines the world over. Some time later I found bags full of my stuff tucked away in the back of a cupboard in my flatmate's room, she had just taken them and stored them like a squirrel in winter. Student life – sordid and splendid. There's nothing quite like it – you're not quite in the world, yet you're not quite out of it either.

UK medical students are given the option of a two- to three-month hospital placement anywhere in the world. We had to fund the trip ourselves, but where we went was a matter of personal choice. The elective is about gaining experience in any aspect of medicine that interests you. You can stay in the UK, you can go to America – somewhere hi-tech, at the forefront of medical technology, or you can go to the third world. I opted for Africa, subconsciously perhaps I really wanted to stretch myself, and I selected one of its remotest regions. I got in touch with the Kenyan Embassy in London and they sent me a list of participating hospitals to choose from. I discovered somewhere that no one had been to before and knew it was the place for me.

And so at the end of my fifth year of medical school Robin and I travelled to Africa, to the Kinango Mission Hospital in Kenya. It was the summer of 1987 and we flew to Nairobi, then took a train to Mombasa. The British had built the railway in 1896, partially as a trade route from Mombasa to the interior and partially to protect their position in Uganda.

Until then the only way in was on foot, a path trodden only by zealots: explorers, missionaries and such like. The railroad was built at a cost of some £5 million, and it blazed a trail through some of the harshest and most hostile terrain in Africa. Not only were the engineers faced with major construction problems – especially in the Rift Valley – but its labourers, mostly indentured from Punjab and Gujarat in India, had the east African wildlife to deal with. They frequently had to face attacks from lions raiding their camps, mauling and sometimes killing them. The railway was dubbed the Lunatic Express. A poem written in the London magazine, *Truth*, in 1896, demonstrates clearly just how little support the project had back in Britain.

What it will cost no words can express
What is its object no brain can suppose
Where it will start from no one can guess,
Where it is going to nobody knows.

The final line of the second verse unequivocally states the popular contemporary view: 'It clearly is naught but a lunatic line.'

And so it was for Robin and I – mostly because we had no idea where we were going or what Africa had in store for us. That first train ride was a real eye opener and should have given us some hint, at least an initial taste of what we were in for. It was like stepping back in time, yet it was other people's time.

As soon as we touched the ground in Nairobi, everybody wanted to touch my hair. It was like a magnet. Wherever I went I had children stroking my head. We stayed in Nairobi that first night and, after sporadic bouts of sleep, we woke early. The sun was just coming up and through the rising mist Africa looked like another world, an old forgotten planet. Under the gaze of a hundred pairs of eyes we made our way to the railway station along a dusty road. It was unnerving, almost threatening, and I was relieved to get there and even more relieved when we finally boarded the train for Mombasa.

Taking the train in Kenya is a fantastic experience. They travel through the night, apparently to avoid the heat of the day. The rolling stock is nearly as old as the line itself. The first-class carriages were built in the 1960s, but the second-class ones date from 1920s' Britain. We travelled second-class, and to my amazement I found myself parted from Robin, segregated in an all-female four-berth carriage. Apart from that there was another immediate problem: one of the women had two children with her, so there were five people to sleep not four. It was crowded in any case, and when I arrived there was a Sunday school picnic going on in the middle of the tiny floor, and Nelly, a Mombasan missionary, was in the process of giving a sermon about Moses. Earplugs would have been wonderful.

I retreated to Robin and the dining car. *En route* I passed the kitchen and thought it somewhat strange when I heard the sound of squawking. I realised it was coming from baskets of live chickens, and the dinner menu that night became instantly apparent. The meal was wonderful though, a vision of silver and white: starched tablecloths, gloved and suited waiters with cotton serving cloths draped over their arms. They worked in a flash of polished cutlery, attending to our every whim, like a scene from *Out of Africa*, filled with the beauty and romance of a continent that has captured the imagination of Europeans for centuries. After supper we headed off to Robin's quarters, which were underoccupied, and I spent the rest of the journey there, chatting to another missionary, this time an American from Nairobi. He had been in Kenya for ten years, and was able to teach me some basic Swahili and point out the wildlife before it got too dark: ostrich, zebra, Thomson's gazelle and rhino. The train passes through the middle of Tsavo National Park, famous for its Big Five – lion, leopard, cheetah, elephant and buffalo – and at some 20,000 square kilometres, it's the largest national park in Kenya. I sat and stared out of the window, watching the back of the train snaking its way across the vast emptiness of the plains. It was a whole other world – a world set back in time.

We pulled into Mombasa at 7.30 the following morning and made our way down to the bus station through another hundred faces, another myriad stares. The station itself occupied one side of a large square lined with stands and benches. There was a sweet, sickly smell in the air, people thronging in every inch of the place. We wandered round a market which sold fruit and leafy green vegetables. The bus for Kinango was not due for a couple of hours so we bought breakfast from a roadside stall: *chai* – a milky sweet tea charged with large quantities of condensed milk, and *mandazi* – a type of doughnut which can either be sweet or savoury. Our hunger satisfied, we wandered among the shops and stalls and watched the life on the street.

We were there as student doctors and our first experience of the health of the people was in that market square. As we stood among the fruit and vegetables a man wheeled himself by in a trolley. I say he was a man, but he appeared to be only half of one with no legs and hardly anything left of his body. He was begging from the shopkeepers and stallholders, but did not approach us. I watched him, crippled, emaciated, hand extended, and knew he was the reason I had come to Africa. I was there to assist in the practice of Western medicine in a country that was largely underdeveloped, where infectious diseases rule as once they had done in the West. Where squalid living conditions, malnutrition and inadequate medical facilities contribute to poor health. Annual public and private health spending in Kenya totals just £5 per person compared with nearly £1,000 in the UK, or over £2,500 in America. The story in other African countries is similar, worse in some. Nigeria spends just over £3 per person on health, Ethiopia just under £2, while Tanzania, which has fewer than one hospital bed per 1,000 people, spends nine times more on servicing its national debt than it does on providing basic health care for its citizens.

The first medical officer to arrive in Nairobi was Dr Henry Boedeker who, quite incredibly, walked with his wife from Mombasa in 1896. When he got to what was effectively still a railway camp, having begun life during the construction of the railroad, he found the terrain swamp-like, with stagnant standing water and mud holes and estuarine vegetation. Swarms of mosquitoes bred and inhabited the area and Boedeker considered it less than a wise choice for an urban centre, though at the time the climate was thought to be healthier than coastal Mombasa. Whether or not it ever really should have, Nairobi grew out of this camp – milepost 327 on the rail track. The soil there did not drain well, and the area became one huge morass of mud. In the dry season it was dusty, the particles of dirt in the atmosphere causing many of the inhabitants to develop a condition known as 'Nairobi throat'.

One hundred or so years later, as we had pulled into stations along the line, brightly dressed children ran up to bid us welcome and ask for sweets. They looked healthy enough. But if you fell ill in a remote region of Africa, there was no hospital to go to, no GP down the road. The quality and range of medical care diminishes fast as you move away from cities, although some rural mission hospitals, like Kinango, have been able to maintain relatively good standards. According to the World Bank there is just one doctor practising for every 10,000 Kenyans. In the USA the ratio is 25 per 10,000, in Germany, 35.

Patients in rural Africa are actually lucky to see a doctor at all. There are non-governmental organisations, such as the African Medical Research Foundation (AMREF), which is based in Nairobi. It was founded in 1957 by three Western surgeons and provides health care to some of the most remote areas in eastern and southern Africa. As well as a flying-doctor service for the region, it tries to fill the gaping holes in local health care by supplying medical skills where needed and by training local staff. AMREF's efforts were recognised in 1999 when they were awarded the $1 million Conrad N. Hilton Humanitarian Prize, the world's richest humanitarian award. The money will go a long way towards helping the health problems of the poorest people in Kenya and its neighbouring African countries, but it will not solve anything long-term.

There is of course traditional medicine: soothsayers and witch doctors to whom many of the local people still instinctively turn. There are medical practitioners who live among their people, and they certainly have experience of the diseases of their region. However, they tend to practise unusual modes of treatment based on local beliefs, while the soothsayers and witch doctors are in another category altogether. When none of that works though, there is nothing left – not unless you can afford the private flying-doctor service, which is out of the question for most of the rural African population.

Most of Mombasa is sited on a coral island in an Indian Ocean bay off the southern coast of Kenya, linked to the mainland at three points as well as by the Likoni Ferry. It is the chief port for Kenya, Uganda and northeast Tanzania. Colonised by the British in 1887, it was the capital of the East African Protectorate until 1907. Kenya's oldest and second largest town, it has a population of about half a million, and owes its development to its location, the island forming a perfect natural harbour. Where we were heading had no such natural advantages, nor any of the benefits you get from a large city.

We took the bus to Kinango at a speed that was far too fast for safety, bouncing over roads pitted with potholes. Our route skirted the Shimba Hills National Park, a small reserve 30 kilometres southwest of Mombasa. It is almost 200 kilometres square, the forest and grasslands, riverine forest and scrub home to giraffe and elephant, leopard and a colony of baboons. It is also the only place in Kenya where you might spot the sable antelope. The strong sea breezes make the hills cooler than the rest of the coast, which means the climate is pleasant.

There is an old Swahili proverb that says a good house is not judged by its door. Just as well, because our house in Kinango had no door. Actually it wasn't even a house – just four brick walls with a sheet of corrugated iron balanced on top to serve as a roof. There was no furniture, no carpet or matting, nothing except the concrete floor. It was a hollow concrete shell. To make matters worse this half-built structure was not even ours. We were to share it with two families, one Japanese, the other American, and (as we were soon to discover) a large colony of bats. I could hear them initially, leathery wings fluttering as they settled upside down on our ceiling. When I finally plucked up courage to look I counted at least 70. Of course they slept during the day, swinging upside down and snoring. This wasn't too bad, but then we weren't there in the daytime. It was the nights that were the real problem – they flew in and out, circling the room in their particularly erratic way for hours at a time.

The bats were one domestic hazard and a visit to the toilet, a long drop at the end of the garden, was another. The bats were not the only creatures out there in the dead of night; the place was crawling with spiders the size of dinner plates, not to mention a multitude of other creepy crawlies. With only a tiny torch to see by, I made a trip to the toilet at night just the once, and that was with Robin by my side to protect me. I tempered my drinking around bedtime after that, so I would not have to venture out after dark at all. But for all that, the African skies were unforgettable. The night was pitch black, and no man made light to disturb a firmament clustered with stars like fragments of chipped crystal.

When we were first shown our accommodation I took one look at Robin, and could see his expression fall as his spirits plummeted. I felt pretty much the same, but could see one redeeming feature – our arrival had coincided with the first mains supply of electricity to the village. Our shack was connected up, but the sum total of power supplied a single bare light bulb that dangled from a flex in the middle of the room. There was no television, no radio, and no hot water. Our washing facilities comprised a bucket of water, fetched from a tap in the centre of the village, while our bathroom was the yard outside the shack. As I already mentioned, the toilet was a long drop, essentially a plank of wood over a hole in the ground: in a word – basic.

But what else could we have expected? Kinango is nothing more than settlements of shacks huddled together at the end of a muddy track. However, the villagers had come out in force to greet us. They were happy people, calm, warm and very welcoming. From the word go, we were made to feel we were part of the village, part of the family. Everyone was extraordinarily friendly and remained so during our time there. Apart from the odd missionary down the years I don't think they had seen many white people, and we must have been a bit of a novelty. The chairman could speak English, along with the more educated among the villagers, but they were few and far between and most of them were illiterate. We could not really communicate verbally with them, so when we wanted conversation we chatted with the mission people or experienced the universal language of play among the children.

The village was larger than I had expected, with a market and several shops. The population then was just under 1,000, and most things you might need were available to buy, including made-to-measure stools and a cycle repair kit. Something that stuck out in particular was the fact that the villagers did not seem to work. There was a lot of milling around, a general hubbub and people sitting in the shade under the trees. The population was tiny considering the vast area their dwellings covered. Many of them were bush folk, the village more of a community centre than a town in the

Western sense of the word. I watched, and I realise now that my eyes were untutored, but nothing much seemed to happen there.

The Kinango Mission Hospital, by way of contrast, was a hive of activity. We visited it on the day we arrived and I was surprised to find it a reasonably sized, relatively clean, well-organised-looking place. We had been engaged to work for the two full-time doctors, Soloman and Tayabali, with the latter man the senior of the two practitioners. We were there to help, and they badly needed whatever help they could get – Soloman and Tayabali were the only doctors in the hospital of 160 beds. These beds were quite often occupied by three people at the same time, not to mention the accompanying relatives and friends sleeping under it. When we did a clinic the queues trailed out of the hospital, down the road and round the corner. People would stand in line for 24 hours at a time to attend one of our surgeries. They would often have walked for a day or more first – journeys of 20 or 30 miles were not uncommon – and if they had not travelled on foot, then they travelled on the backs of bicycles, in bicycle taxis or in rattling old buses. On the whole, the Mission Hospital did not charge for treatment, although sometimes – with organisations such as AMREF – there was a token charge of somewhere between £2 and £4. Even charges as minimal as this are invariably a price too high. In the poorest of rural areas, like that in which Kinango was situated, if a family takes a sick relative to hospital, the rest of its members may well starve. Fearing the bills, many people do not come at all.

When they did come to see us, it was often too late for us to do anything medically helpful, and this was something I found very frustrating. They would have tried all their own remedies long before even thinking about using the facilities of a Western hospital. This was not just because of the costs involved but also because their opinion of Western medicine wasn't very high. By the time we got to examine a patient they were usually very sick indeed.

There *was* a sort of admittance procedure, but it was quite elastic and had very poor records, which obviously we were unable to read anyway. When someone was allocated a bed, they would climb on to it and roll themselves in a vast sarong, head to toe, using the garment like a sheet. As a result, you could never tell how many there were to a bed. There were just these rolls of cloth, and we were never sure which contained bodies and which did not, as you could never see the head, arms or legs.

Unless their families brought in food, the patients would be served the same meals day in, day out. In Kenya the food was generally good: rice, potatoes, chapatis and ugali eaten with chicken, goat or beef as the staple diet. There was an abundance of fruit – mangoes, pineapples and passion fruit – and vegetables, with lots of maize and wonderful avocados, spinach and a cabbage-like green called *sukumawiki*. But hospital food the world over seems to lack imagination, and here it was no different as the patients were served a sort of grey porridge in plastic bowls. It looked distinctly unappetising and was matched in appeal only by the toilet facilities. Most of the patients did not eat the food and would not use the toilets, preferring instead, in the latter instance, to go out into the bush. From the look and smell, and the lack of obvious hygiene, nobody could blame them.

On our first day we had a guided tour of the facilities, which was followed by a ward round. Nothing could have prepared us for the sticky, dirty, sick-people smell that pervaded the wards, made worse by a toxic disinfectant. It was the stench of human decay, there is no smell like it and it made me want to retch. Initially I panicked and thought I could not stay there, but I bit the bullet and quelled the urge to flee and in a few days I got used to it. By the time I came to leave I hardly even noticed it.

The pathology was phenomenal – and gross. Although only one disease, smallpox, has ever been eradicated in the history of man, the diseases here – many that you would find in England – were ten times worse because they had left it so long before coming in for treatment. Some of the local people thought that illnesses were caused by curses, that they were an affliction of an evil spirit or an angry god. So even if we got to them, if relatives had told them that they were going to die anyway, they would sometimes just give up. A lot of the sick had scars all over their bodies – a legacy of the little nicks that they made on their skin at the suggestion of tribal doctors. They would cut themselves either to bleed out the illness or to insert curative herbs and potions. Some of the villagers believed that illnesses had been given to them by their ancestors and that they should wear particular garments to ward them off – in addition to ritual animal sacrifice on the graves of those who had succumbed to disease.

The first afternoon after our arrival I sat in on Dr Tayabali's clinic. It was both fascinating and alarming, covering as it did such a broad spectrum of medicine. From then on Robin and I were expected to take clinics. This proved to be a nightmare. I was still a student with very little practical experience, and my knowledge was extremely limited. Also, I did not speak the language so I could not communicate with the patient to find out about their symptoms, and taking a psychiatric history from a Swahili-speaking patient was virtually impossible for me. Furthermore, there were few facilities. We could do a blood test to check for malaria, but that was about it. When we needed to dress a wound, we often found there were no supplies, and there were hardly any drugs, particularly antibiotics.

So even in those cases where we were able to come to a diagnosis we often had our hands tied. It was awful to see people whose expectation was that we could help them, and then fail them through lack of facilities. I took one book with me, *The Oxford Handbook of Medicine*, a slim tome that covers everything. Robin and I used to thumb through it whenever we were unsure about a patient's condition, trying to fix on something that would help us to make a diagnosis. Assuming we were able to make one, we still faced the hurdle of whether or not there was anything we could do to help. We had no back-up or support. The other doctors were overworked and simply did not have the time. Sometimes it wasn't just the fact that there was little we could do, there were other, less obvious issues. One day while walking the wards I came upon a man crying with pain. The nurses seemed to ignore him and they appeared surprised when I suggested they might try and comfort him. I realised then that I was never going to get used to or understand the way things worked in that remote corner of the world. It was not callousness, it was not even that life was cheap, it was simply a different approach, different realities. Life was lived on the edge, the real edge: nothing was padded or insulated from the brutality of day-to-day survival.

So many sick people slipped through the net. We tried to get patients to wait so we could get a second opinion, but many of them refused and would return home, presumably some to die. For most people we were the end of the line. Every other stone had been turned and there was no one else. Because we were the last resort, despair was a continuing factor, unspoken and unseen in most cases, but still a constant companion, spectral in the shadow of the majority of the patients. It was not so much about individual failures due to lack of resources. It was often wholesale and the entire community would find out about our lack of success, and once that was the word on the grapevine many other people who needed to come and see us would not do so. It was a vicious downward spiralling circle that we could not escape.

True tropical disease has still not been eradicated from East Africa: river blindness is common, specific African types of the HIV infection are rampant, and infections with leprosy and tuberculosis are widespread. Lymphatic filariasis (LF), known more commonly as elephantiasis, or big foot, affects more than 120 million people in 80 poor tropical states with another billion at risk. Mosquito control is not as good as it used to be, hence there is a consequent threat of an increase in malaria. This was something we could treat. Malaria remains one of the major killers in tropical Africa, so it was good to be able to do our bit to help deal with that at least. Someone who was badly affected would be admitted for quinine injections, otherwise we would prescribe Maloprim. People who have been in any malarial region long-term often have a degree of immunity to the disease, and if they contract it their symptoms are not so bad. There are different sorts of malaria – some that only affect blood, two that can lie dormant in the liver, and one that can go to the brain. Essentially you get a recurring fever every few days. It makes you tired and anaemic, and if it reaches the brain it can kill you.

I contracted malaria about three weeks after our arrival. I had taken all the right tablets, but the malarial parasite is becoming increasingly immune to the drugs available to prevent it, even the newest ones on the market. We were in a malarial zone with a high resistance to even the strictest prophylactic regime. Although Robin and I had strung up a pair of large, square mosquito nets from the beams of our room it was impossible to avoid them altogether. I had been bitten mercilessly from day one. I failed to realise it was malaria at first, I just felt a bit under the weather and dismissed it as my body adjusting to the changes in climate, diet and environment. Pretty quickly though I was seriously unwell, a raging fever and rigors, which is how your body shakes and sweats when your temperature gets too high. I am still not sure what type of malaria it was because they did not test for types in Kinango as there were no facilities to do so. However, as I am still here, it must have been one of the varieties that do not stay in your body. In any case I had a narrow escape, not least because they wanted to admit me to the mission hospital. I didn't care how ill I was, liver, brain or whatever, there was no way I was going to share a bed with a trio of mummified buddies or eat grey porridge!

Towards the end of our first week, Robin and I were battling on as best we could, but things got steadily worse, never more so than when we went to work in the operating theatre. As a medical student you do not operate, you might hold a retractor (the metal bookend-shaped wedge that holds the skin and flesh open during an operation) but that is about as much as you are allowed to do. Here it was all hands on deck, and we were expected to operate. If that was not bad enough, the state of the operating theatre had to be seen to be believed. Back in London what we had experienced as a sterile, protected environment, here was a large room with windows and a fan. Flies buzzed everywhere. Some things were familiar though, we were supplied with masks and we wore the usual greens – or at least our hats were green. My trousers and shirt were white, matched by a pair of huge white wellingtons. The clothes were regularly washed, but they were not sterile so wearing them made very little difference.

All the equipment – gloves, needles, syringes – was sterilised and re-used. This was not something with which we were familiar, but it seemed to work satisfactorily for them, for as far as I could ascertain, post-op infection was not especially rife. However, there were more surprises in store. There was no qualified anaesthetist, only the nurses, who took it in turns. At any one time as many as three operations might be going on in the theatres. The nurse responsible for anaesthetics that day would simply go from patient to patient, injecting each of them before going off to the coffee room to have their breakfast while the doctors were left to carry on operating. What was worse was that because there was no diathermy (the electrical tweezers we normally use to stop bleeding points) the operations took much longer than usual, and even longer still because the organisation in the operating theatre was nothing short of chaotic. No one really seemed to know the exact needs of the patient lying on the operating table, which was something I had not come across before and, thankfully, have not come across since.

During the weeks that followed we learned a lot, and learned it quickly. It was an experience that would stand me in good stead. Much later when I joined HEMS, though the facilities and procedures were obviously up to Western standards, I had this vast reservoir of experience to tap into of thinking on my feet.

One of the most common operations we did (after a quick lesson) was to remove a hydrocele, a huge bag of fluid that attaches to a man's testicles but sits inside the scrotum. It is basically a huge cyst, and I mean huge. The most memorable one I saw was in Mombasa, during a visit on one of our weekends off. It was attached to a beggar, and was of such a size that he was sitting at the roadside with a tablecloth over it, using it as a makeshift table from which to sell his wares. Hydrocele are common throughout the world, but in the UK you do not see them of any great size because they are operated on and removed relatively early. But because they are more uncomfortable than life threatening, they are not a medical priority in a country with limited health-care resources. In Kenya I quite often saw people wheeling them round in wheelbarrows to take the weight off them and allow movement. I suppose it helps that the dress code is sarong and not trousers.

A hydrocele in the UK would probably get to about the size of an egg before you operated on it, but the one that we encountered on our first day in the operating theatre was the size of a football. We had watched Dr Tayabali remove one earlier in the day, and he left us to do the next one on our own. We were not used to doing this operation, nor indeed any operation, and consequently were not as quick as either of the other two doctors. My skills as a would-be surgeon were not helped by the huge pair of size seven and a half gloves, the smallest ones available. They were way too big (I wear size sixes) and I was all fingers and thumbs as I tried to work on the patient. Removing a hydrocele is not a dangerous operation, but because we were slow, by the time we cut into it, rolled back the edges, removed the lump and sewed it all back together again, the anaesthetic was beginning to wear off, and our patient was beginning to regain consciousness. In fact he started to jerk as we worked on him, and with the nurse away at breakfast, there was no one to top up the anaesthetic. Imagine it, our first operation – in Africa, working on the most important and sensitive part of the male anatomy and our patient starts to wake up. It was like a scene from a *Carry On* film, but this was real, the room was hot, the dust rose in clouds outside, and flies buzzed habitually. It was a fraught and ghastly moment, and quite how we managed I don't know. But we did, just, somehow.

After this initiation we used to operate fairly regularly on hydroceles, hernias, appendixes and all manner of minor lumps and bumps. Although I found this nerve-wracking to begin with, none of it was major surgery and I soon developed a talent for it. We helped with a Caesarean section once, but never performed one on our own. It all felt a bit shocking at the time, but we got used to it. At least our standards were a little higher than those I read about subsequently, which involved a certain Isaac Misigo, the chairman of Lukembe Circumcisers of Kakamega. He was concerned with improving the professional and ethical standards of his members, something he made clear in a newspaper announcement in 1996 where he listed the new rules by which his members were expected to abide. I had to laugh when I read it, though, unfortunately, it rings ominously true: there was to be no circumcising of dead people, and the person circumcising was to operate only when sober; the tools of the trade were not to be used to threaten others, to repair motor vehicles, nor to castrate dogs; the going rate for the job was Ksh 3000 or £35, or payment in kind was permissible – a cow a reasonable offering in settlement of an account for services rendered.

Robin and I worked wherever they needed us most, which was sometimes in Obstetrics. There we encountered Africa head-on and discovered (what were to us) some very odd practices and the sad stories that accompanied them. For example, if someone in the area had twins they were seen as a witch, so if a woman gave birth at home she would strangle one immediately. If she knew she was having twins, she would try to avoid coming into hospital so that she could do this undetected. We made it a priority to encourage these women into hospital so we could remove one of the twins at birth and foster it out. But our efforts were relatively futile: many would still die.

There were all sorts of local beliefs and superstitions, another of which was how men did not deem a woman worthwhile unless she had undergone natural childbirth. Even if she were likely to die through it, they didn't want us to interfere. There was to be no Caesarean, only natural labour would do. There were all sorts of tragic injustices, superstitions that at best I found frustrating and at worst diabolical. It all served to reinforce the realisation that I would never get used to the way things worked there. Male and female circumcision was commonplace. The ceremony that accompanied the former was an important rite of passage, a huge occasion attended by the whole village at which, if the boy cried or showed pain, he was considered weak and worthless.

Polygamy was still practised, though not officially condoned. The custom of the man taking more than one wife is only recognised in the traditional systems, not by official Kenyan family law. There is a lot of resistance to Western censure of polygamy, but the practice is dying out because of economic realities and social pressure. Few men can now afford to take more than one wife. The Christian Church strongly disapproves but it is not alone. Among the wealthier elements of Kenyan society it is considered an embarrassment when polygamists rub shoulders with the international set. But this was neither a wealthy nor an especially Christian section of Kenyan society. In fact it was a highly promiscuous community, where it was not uncommon for a man to have five or six women.

I got very angry once when attending one of Dr Tayabali's Outpatients clinics. A couple arrived, the woman suffering terribly from the pain of a pelvic inflammatory disease (PID). The husband chatted away merrily, smiling as he told us how miserable his wife was, not giving her one word or gesture of comfort. I felt like kicking him, especially as the chances were that he had passed on the infection himself after sex with another woman.

There must have been a lot of AIDS, although I was not *au fait* with this at the time as medical awareness in the West was not quite on-stream by then. There were certainly a wide variety of sexually transmitted diseases, though not assisted by some of the traditional beliefs. Women were considered useless and consequently were cast out or deserted by their husbands if they were not able to conceive. To get round this some women would try to have a baby by another man. This vicious circle only served to aid the spread of sexually transmitted diseases and the sexual toing and froing did not merely involve the local population. In Outpatients one afternoon a Salvation Army preacher came in, wrongly accusing one of the clinical officers of sleeping with his thirteen-year-old daughter. He ranted and raved, requesting at one point that money be sent to her grandparents so that he wouldn't lose his reputation. However, it was probably all made up, just in an effort to get some money out of the clinical officer. We listened to him for a while, we had to, but we all found it hard to keep a straight face.

But most of it was not funny. I was there before HIV was really in the forefront, and looking back I think I saw an awful lot of HIV that I did not actually identify. But even if I had been able to do so, the facilities to confirm the diagnosis did not exist there. And, in the event that we had been able to come up with a diagnosis, we most likely could not have treated it anyway due to the lack or shortage of the right drugs. There were always shortages of everything. We had a ward round one day when we discovered the hospital had run out of gauze dressings. There was no alternative we could use, we simply left them unchanged. I took an eye clinic another time, only to find that the ophthalmoscope was worse than useless. So little could be changed, certainly not on our elective. Any real changes would take years, requiring not only more funds but, just as importantly, different attitudes. Funding came from the Kenyan government, and the supplies from the city, but sometimes they didn't come at all or took too long to get there. When the supply lorry broke down, which was often, it could not be fixed until there was cash to buy the parts. Our hands were tied and cuffed and the key thrown away. As far as AIDS and other health issues were concerned, it was education more than anything else that was needed to make things better in the long-term. That was going to be difficult, resources or no resources, because education requires trust, and on the whole the local people did not think much of most Western practices or, for that matter, their practitioners.

There were all sorts of other problems to be faced in the provision of health care in that remote part of Kenya, some of them quite mundane and frustratingly easy to solve. Once we set off in the hospital's new Range Rover to operate a mobile clinic, but when we got to the appointed spot, we found no one there because nobody had been told about it. But the flip side to a variety of problems is a whole gamut of new solutions: a memorable one involved a visit from the minister of health. He came to the mission hospital while we were there and the first we knew of it was when the hospital underwent a massive spring clean, followed rapidly by a round to clear the wards, discharging as many people as possible. It was quite extraordinary to witness – by the time the health minister got to see the place it was relatively empty, all for show, for the benefit of politicians. I suppose the upside was that it made our life easier for a few days – until it filled up again after his visit.

There were a lot of stops and starts, however, before the minister of health actually showed up. First he was coming, then he wasn't. It went on like that for days until suddenly one morning Dr Tayabali was summoned to escort the minister from Kwale in the hospital Land Rover. When the minister finally arrived after lunch it was in a VIP entourage that comprised some 40 assorted dignitaries and others – mostly administrators of one sort or another – who proceeded to follow him around on his tour of inspection. It was a huge waste of manpower, of precious resources that could so obviously have been better used elsewhere. During the visit aspects of the hospital and how it was run were looked at and assessed by the visitors – things that had been immediately obvious as wrong to me from the start were pointed out for attention. Those in the firing line were visibly shaking. Whether or not any of the criticisms and suggestions for improvement would be acted on was anybody's guess, though a day or two later we were amused to find some villagers clearing the compound under the instruction of Kinango's headman, Kabweri. They were grumbling a lot, and I do not recall the job ever being finished.

I doubted that anything much would change though some good came of it. Now that the minister had seen the size of the hospital, he was able to allocate it more funding. A regulatory speech had heralded his departure, a political diatribe as far as I could gather, and not at all useful in addressing the real problems that faced Kinango or its hospital. He left very much as he had arrived, with his retinue fanning out behind him, kicking up enormous clouds of dust as they disappeared back to their bureaucratic urban outposts.

I attended all of the clinics during the time I was working at the mission hospital. Sometimes I was left in Outpatients on my own to see patients. Having been given only the barest essentials of a history I was expected to examine them, make a diagnosis and prescribe treatment, or admit them as I deemed fit. I frequently felt way out of my depth, my final recourse being to send most of them for blood smears and to give chloroquine as necessary together with the occasional Panadol or antibiotic. Often the medical officer, a nurse who acted as a doctor, did not seem to know what to do either and was seldom prepared to offer any advice.

In one clinic I had a predominance of babies with whom I could do little, for the simple reason that as soon as I put my stethoscope anywhere near them they bawled their heads off. Many of them were suffering from malnutrition, either protein or total, which was a far greater problem than I could solve. With protein malnutrition the belly balloons, total is total and the victim is reduced to skin and bones. The infant mortality rate is high. Life is tough, assuming you make it beyond birth and infancy.

The nurses tried to help us out as much as they could. In one antenatal clinic we were twiddling our thumbs because there were hardly any patients. To pass the time we started chatting about weight with the nurses. In Kenya it's a sign of prosperity to be fat, so they were all trying to gain weight – the bigger the better. But, while these Kenyan women were attempting to get bigger, they thought it highly amusing that I was trying to stay slim. I would borrow their scales from time to time, watching my weight as I attempted to lose a few kilos. They thought this was highly unusual and quite ridiculous, and cheerfully told me that I needed to fatten myself up, and quickly.

Once or twice Robin and I went on the hospital run to deliver stores and got the chance to see some of the dispensaries. They were very basic, but seemed to do a good job. One day we travelled for two or three hours over to Mazeras along a very muddy road. The driver was incredibly frustrating, refusing to put the Land Rover into 4WD unless we actually got stuck. Consequently we were sliding all over the place. Halfway there we came across a *matatu*, a minibus, that had gone into a ditch, and we had to drive off road to pass it and only just managed to make it through. These were conditions that the medical team at Kinango faced all the time. At each dispensary we were asked to sign the visitor's book, and as far as I could make out we were the first foreigners ever to visit them. This was certainly the case in Mazeras, a truly tropical village, the buildings shadowed by succulently leafed trees at the end of a narrow and winding road.

We also went out with the primary health-care team, who were incredibly disorganised, so much so that they had to devise and write up the questionnaire they were about to distribute from the Land Rover *en route*. There were five members of the team, plus Robin and myself. We all went to each and every house as a group, which was a complete waste of time for a start. Then as we collected the answers to the questionnaire, a member of the team wrote down all the answers themselves, presumably because those questioned didn't know how to write. At least half the time it took to do all this was spent arguing over the age of the respondents and their children. If it had not been so tragic it would have been hilarious. We got wet and muddy tramping from shack to shack, but it was certainly a worthwhile trip if only to witness at first-hand the conditions in which some of the Kenyan villagers were living. Their homes were mostly thatched mud huts that housed up to ten people. There was no ventilation inside and no toilets outside. Drinking water was collected from puddles and streams – it was hardly surprising that health problems were so prevalent.

We worked in Kinango for around six weeks. We were meant to be there longer, but this was as much as we could manage. Although we had learned a lot, it had taken a lot out of us, (malaria included) and even though there was as much work as we wanted to do, we decided one day that we had simply had enough.

Every now and again during the course of that six weeks we needed a break, so we would go to Mombasa or to the beach or the hills at weekends. On one of our days off we trekked to find a Baobab – gigantic trees that can live for 2,000 years. The pods provide seeds that are ground up during droughts to make what is known as 'hunger flour'. The most famous Baobab has a girth of 22 metres and is privileged with presidential protection. Robin could have done with some presidential protection of his own. *En route* to find a Baobab he was mugged, his kagoul stolen, containing his money belt with everything in it: wallet, traveller's cheques and passports. He gave chase, but could not catch his assailant, though he must have scared him enough to drop the money belt. In the course of his pursuit Robin tripped and seriously gashed his knee. It was a deep and nasty cut, but somehow we managed to get to Dr Tayabali's house, where between us we formed the consensus that the cut would not heal unaided and required stitches.

I acted as nurse, and Dr Tayabali sewed the wound using no antiseptic, bar a tube of Savlon, and, more critically, no anaesthetic. Basically he used just a needle and cotton. The needle was not sharp. Robin bit his lip and went very white and at one point I thought he was going to pass out. The next day the wound was very painful, but that was to be expected; however, it did not improve at all during the next few days and then it began to turn septic. We were considering the options – a septic knee was the last thing we needed – when the wound opened up of its own accord and out popped a seed, the source of the problem. No wonder it had turned bad, Robin had fallen victim to the same risks that any of our patients faced given our operating facilities and procedures.

This was not a good couple of weeks for us as it was at this time that I contracted malaria. Robin could not walk without crutches and, as a result, we were not much good at looking after each other. I was more ill than I had ever been in my life, and extremely frightened. I had been relieved when the results of the medical tests came back indicating that I only had malaria and not something much worse or harder to treat such as dengue fever. But I was sick, and still scared and feeling sorry for myself. That was the only occasion in our three months in Africa when I wished I could go home. Given our ongoing circumstances, that was saying something.

After our six weeks in Kinango we went on a month's tour for some much-needed rest and relaxation. So much for that, as we travelled round Kenya and got into some terrible trouble. We lost our way on the upper slopes of Mount Kenya, the 5,199-metre extinct volcano that is Africa's highest mountain. It was the fourth day of a five-day trek. When we should have been on our way down, we were stranded still on our way up, near the summit enshrouded in thick fog without food. If that was not bad enough, a week or so later we spent a terrifying night in a game reserve, our 4WD stuck in the mud of an almost dry riverbed. You don't know man's basic fear till you've been marooned in a truck with the sound of lions roaring barely metres away. Imagine your car breaking down in a Safari park, in the lion enclosure, and the unnerving moments you have to live through while you're waiting for the wardens to come. Imagine that at night with no wardens for miles around and the sound of those lions free, loose and deadly, barely a few metres from where you're cowering.

Mercifully we were rescued in the morning by a passing jeep. As it turned out we were only two miles from the nearest gates of the game reserve but that was two miles too far. These were our low points. We rose above them, but not without testing our luck. We had tried to climb Mount Kenya totally on our own and without any local guides or support, which in hindsight was not very wise. I never did like to do things the easy way.

But Kenya had tested me in other ways, for my fixed views of medicine had been confronted and rudely shaken up. Inevitably one is a product of one's environment and my views were traditional Western ones. They were a combination of coming from the background I did and my inexperience. There were aspects of Kenya, primarily the spirit of its people, which I had enjoyed. But my time in Kinango had made me value what I was about to return to in the UK: the high quality of health care that is available pretty much as a matter of course. It made me appreciate the NHS especially, although this was a view that would later be stretched to the limits. Kenya was as bad as it got (or so I thought). But then at that time I was yet to finish my studies. I had not yet stepped out of medical school into the world of the junior doctor.

4 Houseman in Harlesden

FLYING OVER LONDON AT NIGHT is something I shall remember for the rest of my life. It's a magical sight, the way the city is lit beneath you, around you, sometimes above you, like flying among the stars. I saw it at dusk one evening from the HEMS helicopter after we had accepted a call late in the day. It was dark by the time we had finished. Normally, at that hour the aircraft would have left us to make our own way back to the Royal London by public transport, while it flew on to its hangar in Denham. On this occasion, however, the pilots took us back to Whitechapel before they signed off. We passed over the dome of St Paul's, captured in a halo of spotlights, glimpsed the blue neon glow of the Lloyds Building and the twinkling white triangles that lace the bridges before we descended to the helipad on the roof of the hospital.

London is a fantastic city to live in. I've always thought so, and never more so than the night I'd heard I passed my finals. That night we saw the lights of the city from ground level as we walked the streets after the party we had thrown to celebrate. We were still on a high, ecstatic, the release after months of pressure. Someone suggested we go and see the sights, as if we'd never seen them before. So we did, a group of us including Robin, and we just stared at everything like a bunch of school kids on an outing. Big city, bright lights – I felt dazzled by them. It was such an optimistic time, for each of us the world was our oyster.

I had to pinch myself, not quite able to believe it. I had successfully completed *six* years of medical school. The training to become a doctor is five years, but with my Clinical Pharmacology and Chemical Pathology BSc in the middle of it it was six. I completed two years of pre-clinical training, then took a year out for the BSc followed by the final three years of clinical. Six years in total: it had been a long haul. But as I stood there on the streets of London and considered it all, the feeling of accomplishment was wonderful.

My medical career began as a House Officer (HO) in Vascular Surgery and Orthopaedics at the Central Middlesex Hospital in Harlesden, northwest London – surgery for the first six months, followed by a second six months as an HO in medicine. This is a standard format for houseman training, though not necessarily in that order.

It was August 1988 and twelve months earlier I had been in the heart of Africa working in Kinango, where patients slept three to a bed and Western medicine was the last resort. What a contrast and in some respects what a comparison, only the space of a year and I found myself in one of the roughest parts of London, dodging the cockroaches as I walked down the corridors at night. In Africa I thought I had been thrown in the deep end. In Harlesden the deep end was even deeper and there appeared to be no bottom.

The hospital buildings were old and in dire need of repair and refurbishment. It was quite a depressing place to work not just because it looked so dilapidated, though that didn't help. I looked at the grim walls and peeling paint day in and day out, shift after shift, on call, not on call. The hours house officers put in were ridiculous. If I worked 100 hours a week I was lucky. The fatigue alone was bad enough, but when the fatigue was combined with my inexperience and inadequate supervision, my year at the Central Middlesex became a nightmare. All house officers are by definition inexperienced and they work all the hours God sends. They all suffer from poor supervision and what they anticipated as final year students bears no relation to the reality of that first year. My year was extremely difficult. Nobody and nothing can prepare you for it. If you look at medical students at the end of their final year at medical school and then again twelve months later, I guarantee they will have aged dramatically. What was once youthful and fresh-faced becomes haggard and fatigued and very often disillusioned.

The hours were the killer. Fortunately the rules have changed since I was an HO – they now ensure a maximum 72-hour week for junior doctors – but a decade ago there was no limit. Further pressure is being brought to bear now to reduce the number of hours still more: 56 is the target figure (about half what we did) and I'm not sure how successful a move like that will ultimately be. The hours are onerous, but the upside of being thrown in at the deep end and forced to stay there for lengthy periods is that you learn to swim. One year of house-officer duties and I was far more experienced and confident than I ever thought I would be. My job involved considerable general surgery, and by the end of it I was able to perform minor operations including simple appendectomy and hernia repairs. For the second six months I worked in General Medicine, with a special interest in Respiratory Medicine. I learned how to do practical medical procedures such as pleural aspirate and biopsy, insertion of chest drains, as well as how to manage all common medical emergencies. But I learned all this at a price. It is a question of balance. You need the experience of seeing enough patients but not by working day and night and then all day again. Fatigue brings the obvious and well-documented problems that are hopefully being addressed by the shorter hours.

The number of working hours for hospital doctors has always been a thorny issue. When I was at HEMS the shifts worked by the helicopter pilots were strictly time-regulated. The Civil Aviation Authority is very clear about this, and all pilots have to log everything. If they work one minute over one day, they have to compensate with two minutes off the next. It makes sense: the pilots are responsible for other people's lives, their passengers and the millions of Londoners they fly over and land amongst every day of the year. Fatigue in their profession can kill people, but so can it in mine.

The fact is that there is a double standard in operation, and the HEMS pilots used to get angry on our behalf at how long a day we sometimes had to work. We never thought that much about it – that's what being a doctor is like in the NHS these days. It is the same in most hospitals around the country. What really wore us down, though, was working the day shift as Medic One (the doctor who is first on call) after a night out in the Audi, the operational road arm of HEMS. On an Audi night, in theory, you could be back at the hospital at twelve, but in practice you never are, especially if you respond to a call just before the end of your shift. Even if you do get back at midnight sharp, you still have to empty the packs, sort everything out and lock up. You do not leave the hospital until a quarter to one. With the hour it took me to get back home, I would not be in bed till two, then I'd be up again at six to get in for half past seven the next morning. It was a relentlessly tiring life, work and more work interspersed with little snippets of sleep, but I would not have changed places with anyone. And, for all the stress and pressure and long hours, it was nowhere near as exhausting as my twelve months at the Central Middlesex in Harlesden.

From the start I had a lot of responsibility. These days a houseman has an easier time, and, at least to begin with, they tend to follow the more senior doctors around. They have the time to observe, to look and learn, while our only option was to jump right in. We had to learn the job on the job, and that was very scary. When you combine that kind of pressure with a 100-hour week, our nerves as well as our bodies were shattered.

It was by no means an easy apprenticeship and it was often the little things that caused unexpected trouble. For example, I didn't know how to draw up a drug: the fact that if you do it wrong (like I did the first time) you spray it everywhere. I was also inexperienced at how to put in a drip. In my first week as a houseman I remember being called to someone who had a bowel obstruction and needed a drip inserted in his arm to enable us to rehydrate him. Try as I might, I could not get that drip in: a needle here a needle there – the poor patient was beginning to look like a pin cushion.

The shock to your system is so great during that first week on real duty that nobody will ever be able to explain it. You cannot impart what it feels like. You have just spent five years at medical school where half the time you do not turn up, and it all seems a bit of a game, then suddenly you have responsibility, real responsibility. Life and death situations that you are expected to get on with, be a professional all on your own.

The day I was practising acupuncture on my bowel patient one of the doctors in A&E came and helped me out. I was eternally grateful (not to mention the patient) and after that I used to go down to Casualty and ask them to bail me out whenever I got stuck. They always did. We all pulled together. That was one of the things I learned right away about hospitals. It was a team, and increasingly I realised I enjoyed being a team player.

Initially, though, working in the hospital as a junior doctor was a bit like just having learned to drive. You've passed the test, you're in the car and out for your first spin, then all at once it dawns on you that no one taught you to park.

I was working with orthopaedic cases during my first week: each morning I would do a ward round with my consultant, registrar and senior house officer. Or rather I would tag along behind. Towards the end of this week we were standing in a circle at one end of the ward, tying up a few loose ends. The consultant was deliberating over a female patient who had died a few days earlier, and to my surprise suddenly he turned to me and asked: 'What was the coroner's report on Mrs X?'

My mind raced into overdrive, blind panic for a few moments, then I felt as though I'd driven smack bang into a brick wall as it dawned on me. There was no coroner's report. I hadn't asked for one. All that was left of Mrs X were her ashes.

'I signed the form to cremate her,' I muttered under my breath to my SHO, my immediate superior, who fortuitously was standing next to me. Mrs X had been burned in the hospital crematorium, and I had destroyed the evidence.

I had not realised that certain deaths have to be looked at by the coroner. Some people who die in hospital don't require a coroner's report. This patient had died within two days of an operation, so the rulebook said that she had to be examined by the coroner. All I knew was that when someone died, the hospital's Office – or the people who deal with the deaths within the hospital – phone you up as house officer and ask you to sign the cremation form. We were quite pleased to be asked actually – it was known as 'Ash Cash'. It was only about £25, but we got paid to sign the forms. It sounds heartless but when you're on a houseman's salary, £25 was a lucrative bonus. When Mrs X died I hadn't known any better. They had asked me to sign and I signed, thinking it only a formality.

Fortunately my SHO was a quick-thinking soul. 'Oh the report's not back yet,' he piped up on my behalf. The consultant never mentioned it again.

Houseman? More like housedog'sbody: I worked what is known as a one in two. I did all my normal days and then every other night I had to cover the whole night as well. When I was working nights, it was permissible to sleep in the cell-like room provided, but if I was needed to admit a patient A&E would page me. I used to hate it, not only the interrupted sleep but also the long straight corridor that led from where I slept to Casualty. I would sometimes walk down it at three in the morning, and the cockroaches would scatter across the lino and disappear into the cracks along the edge. It was unpleasant and unexpected – at least to begin with. Once you get used to it you tell yourself it is only to be expected, given the hospital was so old and out of date. Besides, I had seen worse in Africa – just.

I'd been ill in Africa and as if to keep the order of things I fell ill again in Harlesden. Fortunately, it was not malaria this time. I was simply run down and worn out. Initially I had taken a day off with a bladder infection but the consultant I was working for told me that it wasn't a good enough reason to stay off work and that I should just drink more. So I started to drink several litres of fluids a day. By the end of the week I was really ill, a high fever and rigors, the infection having reached my kidney. This time, unlike in Africa, there was no escape from admittance to the hospital as a patient, where I was put on my own ward into a side room where an old lady, one of my own patients, had died the week before.

Of course all the patients knew me because I was their doctor, and most of them had spent a lot of time with me. I was suffering from a severe kidney infection, so I was up and down to the toilet wearing my distinctive elephant night shirt complete with face at the front, ears flapping at the sides and a tail that swung off the back. I don't know what they thought I looked like as I trotted up and down the ward trailing my tail alongside my drip!

I was admitted twice. It did not clear up properly the first time, so I had to go back again. I was in hospital for two or three days, with intravenous antibiotics. I wasn't a good patient, in fact I was badly behaved – all right, very badly behaved. This was partly due to the fact that at that time the hospital would not serve you a vegetarian meal if you were not part of an ethnic minority, which I wasn't. As a nondenominational vegetarian, I became extremely hungry, so when friends came to visit I left with them to eat supper in a local restaurant and returned a couple of hours later with my antibiotic drip still in place.

No sooner was I on my feet again than I was back working those ridiculous hours. During my time as a medical student I had been to the operating theatre to watch, but I rarely saw anything because I'm so small and there was always a ring of people round the body in front of me. Apart from my experiences in Kenya I never operated on anybody until I had qualified. No one ever does: you help, you hold a retractor. You do not do anything invasive, no incisions or anything. As a houseman I did the odd little bit here and there, an appendectomy, a hernia repair, but nothing of any great consequence and I was still a bit green in theatre and not good with blood. The whole experience still made me feel faint, although I do not feel that way any more.

One day we were performing an aortic aneurysm repair on a man – an operation on the big blood vessel that goes down the centre of the body. An aneurysm is a ballooning in the wall of the vessel that, if left, can rupture and lead to death. To repair it the area has to be cut out and grafted back together with a fabric substitute. In order to do this the graft has to be soaked in clotted blood, so that when you allow the blood to run through the aorta it doesn't come squirting out through the sides of the graft. Unfortunately someone had mistakenly soaked the graft in the wrong sort of blood – in heparinised not clotted – the type that stops the blood from clotting. When the clamps were finally released for the blood to flow freely through the newly grafted section of the aorta, it burst through the graft and gushed everywhere. I was holding the retractor, the instrument that keeps the site of the operation open for the surgeon, and I found myself covered in blood. It streamed down my front and soaked through to my underwear. I could feel its sticky warmth oozing over my skin. I did not faint, but I did make a hasty exit. The patient, incidentally, was fine.

The structure of care in a hospital ward generally involves, in ascending order of responsibility, a house officer or HO, in this case me, a Senior House Officer or SHO, a registrar, a senior registrar and a consultant. For some reason there was no registrar in my ladder of authority, so I had just a senior registrar, who was almost a consultant and did not come in often, much like the consultant. There was no middle-grade doctor, and I, the most junior member of the team, found myself with the responsibility for a ward of 30 patients during my first six months as a doctor. It was just the way it was and I had no option but to deal with it. But to call the situation stressful would be an understatement, and for a significant percentage of the time I went about my work petrified that I'd do something wrong.

There were lighter sides to it all though, such as the time I had to insert a catheter into a young male patient. I had missed that male anatomy session at St Mary's, but I knew roughly what to do. Some things, however, they can never teach you at medical school, however conscientious you are about turning up to class. As I was performing this little procedure, to my horror, the patient started to become aroused. I did not know whether I should carry on shoving the catheter in and pretend I hadn't noticed, or just leave it. My mind went into a spin. I have rarely felt so embarrassed – and from the look of him, neither had the patient. I went on for a little longer then made some excuse about an urgent case and swished out through the curtains, telling him as I went that I would send in someone else to see him. Surprisingly enough I still don't like fitting catheters in men!

It is one of those strange irregularities in medical etiquette. No male doctor or nurse is permitted to perform intimate medical procedures on a woman without a chaperone, but female doctors and nurses are allowed to attend to men on their own. I suspect it is an historic anomaly, but one that will probably be changed in the future.

*   *   *

Just after I qualified I bought my flat in Queen's Park. I still live there, but I bought it with a friend from my year at medical school. We knew each other well enough and decided on this course of action because we were tired of moving house and being shunted around. We also thought it would be a good investment. The plan was that I would live there for the first six months, while he was doing his housemanship in a hospital somewhere up north, and then he would move back to London while I went to Bath for my second house job. While he was away I was to rent out his room to help pay the mortgage. This I did eventually, to someone I met at a party.

It was at a birthday celebration. David was an Australian lawyer, who was staying with the hosts. In fact he was only half-Australian, in the sense that he possessed an English passport, but he had lived most of his life in Melbourne, where he was born. He was working for the law firm, Nabarro Nathanson, in London, but he had also owned a pizza restaurant back in Melbourne. We spent most of the evening chatting, and we seemed to get on well. Afterwards it was reported back to me that David had said, 'She's absolutely lovely, but she's too short to be fanciable.'

That suited me. I wanted a lodger not a boyfriend, and offered David my spare room. He accepted my offer and moved in the following weekend. The room itself was almost as bare as our accommodation had been in Kinango: no home comforts and no furnishings. His bed was a mattress on the floor, but David was happy enough.

He was 30 when I met him, I was 24. I still do not know why or how I went on to marry him, but that's exactly what I did. We got together after David moved in and he proposed when he'd known me for about three months, which I suppose is not long. But I had decided that if I were to get married I wanted to do so while it was all still exciting. Looking back it *was* impulsive – a very Arian trait. I had no idea he was going to propose. I used to wear a ring that my sister had given me on the fourth finger of my right hand, and he removed it while I was asleep one night. Using that as a guide for the size, he commissioned a solitaire ring from a jeweller in Hatton Garden and gave it to me after we went to see the Royal Ballet at the Royal Opera House. Romeo and Juliet: he knew I loved ballet.

We had got stuck in traffic, so we missed the start and had to watch the first half on close-circuit TV in an anteroom. That cast a bit of a shadow over the evening, but afterwards David made up for it by taking me to dinner at Inigo Jones in Covent Garden. It was an expensive, fashionable West End restaurant, but not exactly intimate, especially as our table was right next to a huge party of Americans. It was not in the least romantic when he got out the ring and asked, 'Will you marry me?' Our American neighbours were listening in; I could hear them whispering, 'Oh, he's asked her to marry him. Ooh, she's said, "Yes."'

From the start nothing was quite right. I remember vividly walking back to the car and thinking, I've just got engaged and that means I'm going to get married – is that really what I want? He had just so shocked me by producing that ring. I don't think I was in love with him, but I was completely overawed by him, his good looks, his charm, his witty repartee. On top of that, like me he had a profession and, as a lawyer, he was solvent and earning good money. He had everything – at least he did on paper.

As soon as I got home, which was around half twelve, one o'clock maybe, I phoned my mother to tell her the news.

'What?' It was not a delighted exclamation. No great pleasure in her voice. In fact there was very little enthusiasm at all. I felt even more apprehensive. My family had met David, and they really liked him, but my mother thought it was too soon. Why rush into things? she had asked, as mothers are wont to do. From the start she believed it would be a difficult marriage: we were both professional people and neither one of us would have time enough for the other. 'He's going to want you to look after him, and you're going to want him to look after you. I don't think it will work,' she said a week after the engagement. It's funny how mums have a habit of knowing best.

It was all a mistake, and by the time I got married to him I knew I shouldn't be doing it. It wasn't just him: I should not have been marrying anyone at that point in my life. We did discuss it, but his family in Australia had their flights booked to come over so we went ahead anyway. Strange how people do things like that, make life-changing decisions because a few people have aircraft tickets booked.

We were married within nine months of meeting one another, in Bristol, a white wedding in a very old church in Failand. Like true Aussies, his family wore top hats with corks on strings dangling from the brim, and they decorated the Gothic arch that led into the church with boomerangs. I had a terrible chest infection. I coughed and spluttered throughout the service, so much so that somebody at the back was heard to say, 'For goodness' sake, why don't they send that person out?' The vicar kept asking me, 'Can I get you a drink? Water? Would you like something stiffer?' I was really struggling. I was so ill. It was something of an omen, just another one of many.

We went to DisneyWorld in Florida for a week, followed by a week in St Lucia where we found ourselves honeymooning in the eye of a hurricane. When we got home, it was the tail end of my houseman year. I was working 13-hour days and David's day was not short either – he was often in the office from nine in the morning to seven o'clock at night. We both had incredibly busy working lives, and there was no time to spend together. I did not know him well at all: in many ways I never did. When he was nice he was lovely, but he had a terrible temper. I remember we were driving somewhere, and I had misread the directions. He just hit the roof, started slamming the windscreen. All I had done was to send him down a wrong turn.

I had met David just as I had started my houseman year, and I stayed in London because of him, abandoning my plan to go to Bath for the second six months. I remained at the Central Middlesex, while the friend with whom I co-owned the flat stayed up north, because he had met someone too. When it comes to a houseman post you can virtually choose where you want to go, but when I had finished that six months I was not sure what I wanted. I decided to apply for a position in Accident and Emergency (A&E), a career progression that a lot of us follow in medicine. It would be my first SHO job, the level at which I could expect to remain for the next three or four years.

I was appointed to a six-month posting in the casualty department of Hillingdon Hospital in northwest London. The hospital sits on the edge of the M25, and is even busier because the A40 and the M4 intersections ensure that it serves as the first port of call for road traffic accidents (RTAs). Heathrow Airport is nearby, so Hillingdon has to deal with casualties from there too. I had one patient who had been brought in after falling ill in Terminal 1. They suspected it was something to do with drugs, and as this was always something we looked out for we X-rayed the man's abdomen. Studying the X-ray it was not difficult to come up with a diagnosis: no normal intestine that I've seen contains a row of small plastic bags. He had swallowed a huge quantity of heroin, enough in just one of those bags to kill him if it split. On this occasion the bag hadn't split and the patient was fine: no doubt he's languishing in jail somewhere now, or has died in a similar, repeated attempt at drug smuggling.

Once again I was working hundreds of hours, over twelve hours a day. I had just got married and I was working four out of five weekends, then my shift would change to a week of nights: not a recipe for a happy marriage. It was incredibly hard work but I absolutely loved it. I really began to enjoy medicine. My very first week was nights, which meant I was the only doctor covering the entire A&E Department. I was responsible for anyone that came in. In some ways this was scary, but I had a lot of backup from a lot of brilliant nurses. They baby-sat me through it, helping me, advising me to do this or that. Nurses in A&E are generally very experienced and frequently know more than you do when you start. Good doctors respect and listen to them, and between them they get you through it.

I was living with David in the flat in Queen's Park and commuting to Hillingdon, which was fine when I was on days, because I was going against the traffic. But when I worked nights I was going out and coming back during rush hour. It used to take me about an hour and a half each night and morning, but I didn't really care because now I had found my niche. I liked the speed at which everything happened, the buzz, the rush, the surge of adrenaline, and the fact that no two days were the same.

I had one case of a man who told me he had slipped and fallen on an apple. Whether that was what he had actually done only he would be able to tell you, but he most certainly had an apple stuck up his bottom. Somehow we had to remove it. He was lying on the bed curled up on one side and I was using a vaginal speculum to take it out. It was a Granny Smith apple, green and no doubt sharp. As I stood working away behind him, my shoulders were jiggling up and down, my body shaking I was laughing so much. We could not get it out whole and had to break it down into bits, segments, chunks of Granny Smith, bit by bit, slice by slice. You get all sorts of bizarre moments in A&E, but that was my first apple in the bottom, and so far it's been my only one.

My first week at Hillingdon I was too scared of the responsibility to appreciate the buzz that gradually becomes addictive. By the end of the week I felt as though I had started settling in. My consultant, Pam Nash, was a woman, and she was fantastic. She was my very first role model, the doctor I admired most out of all the doctors I had encountered during my seven years being around them. I thought I would like to be like her. Only in her early 30s, she had just started in the consultant's post, having been one of the senior doctors in Casualty at the Central Middlesex when I was houseman there. When she moved to Hillingdon she invited me to go with her, offering me the job in A&E. She was a superb doctor, dynamic, keen, very kind and very human.

It was an inspiring six months but unfortunately tragically marred. There were seven of us Casualty Officers, working the department in shifts, and we became friends as well as colleagues. There was one doctor who tended to keep to himself. He never said very much, but if you were tired or needed a break he was always the first to notice: he would encourage you to go and have a cup of tea or sit down for a few minutes. One of his relatives died soon after I joined, and I remember that he had time off for the funeral. He was away for two or three weeks and when he came back he seemed fine. We were all sympathetic, telling him to let us know if there was anything we could do to help. Sometimes the random nature of life has a cruelty all of its own, and that year it seemed that way for our friend. Not long after the death of his relative he found out that he had a serious illness. Once again we were all very understanding and we reassured him as best we could.

One week later our consultant called a meeting: she arrived, deeply upset. Our colleague had taken his own life. When his body was discovered they found a note he had left requesting that he should not be taken to Hillingdon Hospital Casualty Department because the doctors there would be really upset as they knew him. It was extremely distressing for all of us, someone you worked with, someone you felt you knew even if only a little. Quiet people are always the most difficult to fathom. It was extraordinary that even when he was contemplating suicide he was still selfless enough to consider us.

I remember feeling terribly guilty afterwards – guilty that I'd failed to notice anything, the deteriorating state of his mind. It was only later that we discovered the true depth of his depression. His relative wasn't dead at all. Our colleague had used his supposed demise as an excuse because he had felt too depressed to face coming to work. He simply could not cope. There was a memorial service for him later and all of us attended. It was all so very sad – a tragic waste of a kind and lovely man. His death touched us deeply, having a profound effect on all of us. But it was private, a shared grief that those we encountered in a professional capacity could not and would not perceive. We were doctors. Doctors deal with death all the time. The phone still rings. The ambulances still arrive. We dug deep and we got on. That was our survival mechanism.

In a team like the one at Hillingdon we all know each other very well and we look after one another. It's a tight-knit community but sometimes someone slips through the net like that doctor did. He had a certain reserve but he was as friendly as the rest of us; we were all always extremely busy so we never knew. We never had time to know. People who are really depressed do not show it. This applies particularly when they are planning to kill themselves, because they don't want anyone to suspect and try to stop them. They internalise their problems, lock them away; they are not able to communicate their distress, which only makes it worse. We were all subject to great stress and strain, but although the external pressures of the job on top of his internal suffering probably did not help, I don't believe his psychological distress was caused by his work.

Working in A&E was tough, RTAs coming in, people smashed and maimed and suffering. There were other sad cases. I had one, a young baby who was extremely ill with meningitis. When the parents brought it in we saw the telltale purpuric rash and knew what was wrong right away. Meningitis progresses quickly so you need to act immediately. If you don't catch it in time it can be fatal. It can start with a couple of specks of red, and within an hour the rash can be all over the body: it is so swift it's scary. We put up drips, gave fluids and antibiotics to deal with the infection, desperately trying to save the baby's life.

When you treat a baby it's difficult to wear gloves because you are not able to feel the veins since they are so small. We were dealing with meningitis and had no reason to suspect there were any other dangers. I was working with two other doctors and there were several nurses involved. There was blood everywhere: it was a real mess.

These days, with the threat of AIDS, it is very important that you wear gloves when treating a patient. Back then it was not such a big issue, particularly because we were dealing with a baby. However, it is now something all medical staff are vigilant about.

I had my share of the more mundane things during those six months too: the ankle strains, the stubbed toes, the coughs and colds, before I took up my next SHO post at Charing Cross Hospital in London. I did a year of anaesthetics, which was the next step along an A&E career path, and took my Diploma of Anaesthesia at the end of it. I did not go on to qualify as an anaesthetist, but I can put somebody to sleep, as I had to do at the roadside when I was working for HEMS. When you specialise as an anaesthetist you start from scratch, right from the very beginning, as if you had not covered anaesthetics at all as a medical student. It is a medical speciality: in practice, a slightly macabre mixture of boredom and fear.

Putting the patient to sleep is the interesting bit: once you've done that all that's required of you is to keep a check on them while waiting for the operation to be completed. Half the time you are bored stiff: you stand vigil with the monitor going, *blip, blip, blip*; documenting their pulse and blood pressure every so often. I used to walk round the operating theatre, practising my dance steps I would get so bored. By then I had started doing Ballroom and Latin American, so I practised those the most.

The other side of the coin, of course, is when things go wrong: such as when you have difficulty inserting an endotracheal tube and the patient begins to turn blue due to lack of oxygen. I had such an incident with a baby when I was very junior. I was unable to ventilate the lungs with my bag and mask – probably because in young children the tongue is relatively big and can sometimes block the airway. In any case the black rubber mask covered a lot of the baby's face, but left enough of it exposed for me to see that the skin was dark blue. I started to panic and immediately called for help. Backup came in the shape of an ODA, the Operating Department Assistant, who is highly trained in helping the anaesthetist. Fortunately I had a very experienced ODA that day – he took over and swiftly stabilised the baby. Boredom and fear: abject fear. I was fortunate that day, but for a moment it was terrifying. It's the kind of fear that sets your heart pounding and the pulse throbs painfully at your temple. You have three minutes before the lack of oxygen will begin to cause brain damage. After that it's anybody's guess. Cold can buy you extra time, as the brain metabolism slows down – that's why people who have drowned or been immersed in really cold water can sometimes be successfully resuscitated much later on. In hospital surgeons sometimes use a hypothermic technique, where they actually lower the body temperature to help make the operation safer and give them more time.

Half terror, half boredom: either way I couldn't handle it. I used to wake up in the night and think that I had fallen asleep during an operation; that I had forgotten the patient and in my half-awake state I'd think that David was the patient, and I'd let him die.

The anaesthetists' diploma taken at the end of the year involves a whole day of exams: multiple choice, written and viva. Results are announced the same day in the Royal College of Anaesthetists on Gower Street. When you arrive you are ushered into a huge hall where you stand and wait until two big doors open, and one of the examiners emerges to read out the numbers of those who have passed. It was a horrible ten minutes in which my heart was in my mouth. Waiting for the results was scarier than actually doing the exam, and for me that is saying something. There is a side of the medical profession, an aspect of its rituals, that almost contrives to embarrass you, to humiliate you before letting you in like a weird kind of initiation ceremony. There is an element of public school about it. It would have been easier just to put a list of those who had passed on the wall so that it wasn't quite so obvious who the failures were. But if you are successful and your number gets read out, it is a very proud moment to pass through those vast double doors and be greeted by a handshake and a glass of sherry. I know because I passed, and sailed through to meet my examiners with a big smile.

Medicine can still be very old school, very traditional. I have never felt discriminated against because I'm a woman, but there are areas of the profession that are not exactly female friendly. There are stories of young female medical students being told by well-meaning consultants that they would never be able to have a family if they went into surgery, and that if they did, they would not get a career post. More recently, provisions have been made for women to forge both a successful career and a family life.

Surgery is generally acknowledged to be the most lucrative branch of medicine, with huge scope for work in the private sector. It is also considered the most prestigious and remains the profession's last male stronghold. Only 5 per cent of Britain's 4,190 surgeons are female, with the gender ratio varying between specialities. In orthopaedic surgery, for example, less than one per cent of the surgeons are women. This is a sobering thought indeed when you consider that at least half of all medical students are female. In autumn 1999 the Royal College of Surgeons came clean and acknowledged surgery as the last male bastion of the medical profession. It is a notorious male club, old school, but not to the extent that it could not admit it has new targets for recruiting women into surgery. It says that by 2004 one in ten surgeons working in Britain should be female, rising to one in five by 2009.

The fact is that surgery is a hard choice for women, and most of us choose not to do it because of the commitment involved or, rather, expected. Because of the lack of encouragement, partly from those in the upper echelons of the profession who are not generally interested in recruiting women, we tend to dismiss it as an option early on. What woman would want to work in a cut-throat environment, where the surgical culture encourages a tough attitude to trainees, with those deemed unfit culled at every stage? And once you have made it, there are the expectations of those in charge: complete dedication, that you will work extremely long hours, much longer than in other branches of medicine. They have made it a male preserve, a sort of macho specialism, where only real men hold the knife, and they have ensured the financial rewards are unparalleled.

I never had any desire to take up surgery, so I did not feel thwarted. My aim was true and A&E was my goal. But life at this point was not all plain sailing. Three years into our marriage David was offered a job in Dubai. We talked about it, and despite my objections he decided to accept it, with a view to me eventually joining him there. I was extremely busy, not only at work, but also dancing, having taken up ballroom after my houseman year. I would go to a dance class whenever I had any free time. I was dancing for fun, but it was pulling me in slowly but surely, and just after David left for Dubai I started doing mini-competitions.

It was giving me ideas, but I thought dancing was only a distraction and dismissed it as such. I could never earn my living from it: not now I was a doctor.

After my year of Anaesthetics at Charing Cross I stayed on to do six months as an SHO in the A&E department. As a senior SHO, I was now a rung above the SHOs who had just finished their house jobs and enjoyed teaching them where I could. I felt I was making good progress, and between autumn 1991 and the following winter I did a variety of locum appointments. I was still on line for a career in A&E, though I now needed more experience in orthopaedic surgery. With this in mind, I applied for a job in that speciality at St Peter's Hospital in Chertsey. The post was due to commence in March and, while waiting for it to begin, I filled my time by going to Central America for a two-and-half-month holiday. I travelled round Guatemala, Mexico and Belize, thoroughly enjoying myself and anticipating the future. There had been a lot of changes in my life so far, but maybe this was an end to it. Perhaps at last I was settled on my course with good weather, calm seas and a fair wind behind me.

5 Trading Places

I FREELY ADMIT TO LEADING a double life for a while. For a few
years I had managed as Dr Heather Clark, and then all of
a sudden something inside me snapped. I think I actually
reached the beginning of this point close to the end of my
houseman year, but it built and built over the next couple of
years and then all at once it exploded. By then I had begun
to equate a life in medicine with a life unfulfilled. Although I
knew that if I stayed it would be in the field of A&E, I
nevertheless felt like I was on a treadmill and I reached the
point where I realised I had to get off. There was a yearning
in my soul, a yearning born of old. I longed to dance again.

It is quite possible that the pressures of the job were more
to blame than anything inherently tedious about work as a
doctor. When I first began to have doubts I had reached the
end of a horrendous twelve months, where 100-hour weeks
had been the norm. I was doing nothing but work. Quite
literally, I didn't even have time to go out at lunch and have
something to eat. I knew this would be the pattern for the
next three years and I was not at all happy about it.

It was a turning point, a sort of crunch time. I thought long
and hard and decided that at 24 I was too old to return to
ballet and reach, never mind exceed, the standard I had
achieved during my late teens. That had been my prime, and

whatever I did with ballet now would be a backward step, offering me no challenge and nothing to aim for.

So I picked something completely different and opted for ballroom and Latin dancing. For the next two or three years I devoted every spare waking minute to the waltz and the foxtrot, to the rumba, jive and cha cha cha. This was not at the expense of my career as a doctor – not to begin with at least. But I have no doubt it initiated the seams of separation in the already flimsy structure of my marriage.

My decision to pursue ballroom and Latin had been partly inspired by the parent of a friend who had danced with me in the Bristol Light Opera Company. She was a ballroom fanatic and would talk about little other than the ballroom and Latin competitions she used to dance with her husband. She had a passion for life that matched mine, and whenever we met at parties she and I would dance together. There was an inspiration, a spark and verve and magic about it for us: it was in our blood.

Once I had made up my mind to take it up again, I phoned round a few places and located the Christine Haynes School of Dancing. This was a small venue just round the corner from where I lived, a dance floor over the top of some shops on Kilburn High Road. I started to go for group lessons on evenings I wasn't working, and I absolutely loved it. They had party nights, and it was great fun. I found the dances very easy, largely because of my ballet training, and I picked them up faster than anybody else. I was used to learning steps, it had been part of my experience since childhood. The problem with this eventually, however, was that it was not enough of a challenge for me. It wasn't long before I started to feel held back, that everybody else was taking it too slowly and lacking the ambition to go further.

There was also a major problem with men. There were just not enough of them. Ballroom dancing is not a popular male pursuit so, unless you were happy to dance with girls, there was always a shortage of partners. This was fine for Latin, but not something that worked well with ballroom.

I had a few private lessons as I thought that perhaps this would push me on a bit. I did my first few exams, the bronze and silver medals in both ballroom and Latin, which were held at the school and judged by an external examiner. I found them easy and got good marks in both. I also did some Medallists' competitions, the most junior of junior competitions you enter when you're just beginning your career. I danced with a lady called Janet, who was short like me. She took the male role, as she had done more dancing than I had and didn't find it a problem to swap positions.

Glen was another teacher I had at that time: he taught at a dance school in Turnham Green that I had begun to attend. He was superb, but eventually he left because he railed against the image that surrounds much of competitive dance. He felt it had moved away from its roots, concentrating too heavily on the look, especially Latin dancing. Spiky fingers and vapid faces with fixed and plastic smiles: it had all become forced and unnatural, almost a little kitsch. In some ways I agreed with him, but not enough to put me off, though I did find certain aspects of the dance world just as hidebound and hyperbolic as portrayed in the movie, *Strictly Ballroom*, though lacking its sense of irony.

Dance was not the only string to my bow, but I still wanted it to be fulfilling, and I was finding that neither the local dance school nor my private lessons were giving me the challenge or excitement I craved. I needed to go that extra mile. Fortunately someone told me about the Moon Glow Dance Studio in Watford, which specialised in training dancers for all bands of competition. I began lessons there, and once they had an idea of my level of ability they helped to find me a partner to dance with competitively. Thai Pham was a Japanese-American computer-programmer, working for his American employers in London. He was a little older but not much taller than me. At 5 foot and three-quarters of an inch I needed a short partner, preferably not taller than five foot seven. Even then, three-inch heels notwithstanding,

I still tend to be kicked by my partner in the crutch every time he swings his leg.

With ballroom dancing the look is everything. The image you create as a couple is central not only to your everyday dancing but also, crucially, to how you fare in competition. You have to fit with the other person. This was not a problem for us – Thai and I fitted perfectly as a couple. The real issue was that Thai, though handsome, did not look ballroom. He was stocky, with a short neck as oppose to the lean and hungry look. Ideally that should be combined with a haughty, almost disdainful air. It was not just Thai. I was not ideal either. The women needed to be tall and willowy, impassive. I am small, lithe and lively, far more Latin than ballroom.

Thai was a lovely guy and a fanatic about ballroom. He loved it with a passion and had been dancing for years. I, on the other hand, was an absolute beginner. He decided, nevertheless, that he would take a chance on me, and so we began to take lessons together, to practise working on the way we danced as a pair. I caught him up rapidly. He knew all the steps and the names of each part of each one, could recite them like a mantra – Natural Top, Opening Out, Sliding Doors, Rope Spin – none of which I had any knowledge of, but his technique was in need of some refinement.

We took part in our first competition only a few weeks after first dancing together. It was at the Rivoli Ballroom, in Brockley, southeast London. This is one of the most beautiful ballrooms I have ever seen: dancing there is like stepping back in time, it's like revisiting *The Age of Innocence.* From the outside it looks decidedly unpromising – yellowing, flaky paintwork, crumbly in places – but inside it's like walking on to a Hollywood film set in the thirties. The ballroom itself is long and hung with crystal chandeliers that glimmer and sparkle, huge against the ceiling. Everything is red velvet and gold trim, strings of fairy lights surround the bandstand. The whole place seems to shimmer like an oasis in the desert. I still go there to practise sometimes even now, and I love it.

It is majestic and low key in the same breathless moment. There's a resident dog and a cat that wander, with an air of quiet nonchalance befitting such a setting, among the dancers as they practise. It is an enchanted place, the stuff of fantasy. But it is still very much a working establishment. There are tea dances several times a week, afternoons and evenings, and people come from miles around. There are dance classes for ballroom, jive and Latin, and the BBC are always filming there – most recently footage for a health education promotion, featuring Thora Hird encouraging us to take more exercise.

As I drove down from north London with Thai, I was bubbling with a cocktail of excitement and apprehension. We crossed the river at Tower Bridge; the Thames sparkled, and the world seemed full of hope and promise. I don't think I'm happier than when I face a new frontier. This was a new dawn for me, another fresh beginning, my first competition at this level, and I had bought a second-hand dress especially for the occasion. Like the dance hall itself the dress was luxuriant, a snowball of white tulle with spaghetti thin straps, a fitted bodice studded with sequins and gold glitter. Attached to the two-tiered, ankle-length, accordion pleated meringue of a skirt, was what resembled a flock of canaries. In fact they were just tufts of yellow feathers. I felt absolutely marvellous in that dress, full of fire and life and ability. Thai wore a white-tie tuxedo, as did all the male dancers. These are cut in a very special way with a triangular slice of fabric stitched into the sleeve under the arms. This insert enables the dancers to move their arms up and down, and ensures that the line of the jacket across the shoulders stays smooth when they do so. Visually, the arms have to align horizontally. The look is everything.

I was so nervous, almost trembling with anticipation. I had changed in the cloakrooms that lined the entrance foyer and sat around ready and waiting for what seemed an eternity. At last though our turn came and when I positioned myself to take up hold, my arms were shaking and my legs wobbled like jelly. People watched from the tables edging the floor, most of them other competitors. There are various categories and we were flushed through three or four heats and into the final round, after that it was in the lap of the gods and judges. We danced our final performance and waited, sweating, nervous with excitement and weariness. This was our very first competition and I waited for those judges with bated breath. At last the results were called and incredibly our number was among them. I was delighted, over the moon. We had won our very first competition.

It was wonderful, could only augur well for the future and it completely affirmed the initial resolve to revive my dancing.

Of course other things were happening in my life, not just the dancing. I focused on that because it was the foil I wanted and needed for what was happening to me medically, the unholy hours I kept as a junior doctor. Dancing and working were just about manageable, but my marriage didn't seem to be adjusting too well to this new lease of life. David had two left feet, or so he said, and he refused point blank to join me on the dance floor. This was understandable, but what was more difficult was the fact was David did not like me attending dance class at all. He did not want me to spend so much of my already limited free time away from him, and was jealous of my dancing with other men. I was not romantically involved with my partner at all; we were just good friends. But it's true to say dancing has an intimate element to it. Certainly, when you are ballroom dancing you cannot avoid body contact because you are in touch physically the whole time. And then there is Latin, which is tricky in other ways, because it is sensual and seductive by its very nature. I can understand why David did not like it very much. But I was not prepared to give it up, and he never came along to any of my rehearsals or competitive events. This did two things: it meant that we saw even less of each other, and equally he had no idea of the innocence of what I was doing. He did nothing to allay any of his own fears, and I felt as though I was in it on my own with no support from my partner. Our relationship – our marriage – was beginning to flag and none of this was helping.

We lived in my flat all the time he was in London. We never owned anything together. We never had one joint possession. And when we got divorced not long after, there was nothing to split between us. Our relationship had never felt like a marriage.

It didn't end that badly in one sense at least since we actually got divorced when David was in Dubai. Two years after he left to take up the position he was still there and I was still here. There was no bitterness. There were no children's lives involved. It just happened: we split properly and finally. I do think that even if he hadn't moved abroad we would have split up anyway, but it probably would have been much more emotional. So in a way I think I got off lightly. I never asked for anything. I didn't want any of his money. He didn't want any of mine. There was nothing to be settled financially. As a lawyer he did all the paperwork: I just signed it, and that was it. In fact his best man delivered the divorce papers to me. David recently remarried and is now a father. He still lives in Dubai, but he packed up being a lawyer and started his own businesses. Notwithstanding the relative ease of unravelling it all, I have been wary of relationships since. I'm far from cynical but I do believe I shall take my time, think long and hard, and be very sure of myself, my circumstances and my partner before I get married again.

In some ways it was a relief when David went to Dubai. I felt free again. There was nobody to hassle me, nobody to question me. I could dance as much as I wanted, and by this time it was usually twice a week. Being me, I was heavily involved in the dancing, but equally being me, my work as a doctor did not suffer. Quite the contrary in fact, I've always thought it makes for a healthier approach to your work if you have strong outside interests.

I had just started my third medal exams before David left, and I did not enter a competition until he had gone to the Middle East. But after our first rush of success, our victory at the Rivoli, I never again won a ballroom competition with Thai. It might sound odd after that initial success, but we tended to be better at Latin. The only problem with Latin dance is the outfits – the revealing next-to-nothing dresses you are expected to wear in performance. One of my outfits was a black bikini, the bra top of which was studded with diamanté and fringed with tassels, the lower half, edged in a calf-length fringe of long black tassels, with a low-slung silver diamanté-embroidered belt along the top. The Latin dress code for feet was high-heeled open-toed sandals with a T-bar and ankle strap. The ones I wore with that bikini outfit were made of fake snakeskin and diamanté!

Thai was the proverbial Man in Black, but at least his body was covered up. Most of mine was on show, and it was Latin so I could not be pale. I used tubes and tubes of fake tan over the years, I should have had shares in the stuff! I will always associate that smell (like acid drops and vanilla) with the Rivoli and the other ballrooms I visited over the next few years: every Winter Garden from Blackpool to Bournemouth. None of this glamour and glitter was as important at this low level of competition. I would just slap on some make-up in the dressing room or cloakroom, a dash of lipstick and not much else, with my hair pulled back in a bun or French plait. Later on I had to take it more seriously, the level was tougher and the look more intricate and extravagant. I did not really appreciate how important this was until I started to do more high-level competing. Then we had to look perfect. My make-up took half an hour to apply: layers of foundation and powder, lines and lines of mascara and thick glossy lipstick. My hands were carefully manicured with long, immaculately varnished nails. We dressed to thrill and we dressed to kill. And kill is exactly what the shoes did to your feet. Ballroom court shoes are a nightmare with their three-inch heels and pointy toes. I had a bunion when I started, and by the time I finished, especially after practising all night, I could barely walk.

While I was dancing with Thai, we took part in an amateur competition at a dilapidated dance hall in Southall. On this occasion we did not do well: we came third in Latin and nowhere in ballroom. But it was an interesting day in other respects, not least because of a demonstration by Philip Banyer and Michelle Green – one of the UK's top amateur-dance pairs at that time. Philip and Thai went back a long way. They had first met at the Moon Glow, and towards the end of the evening they spent a lot of time chatting. Afterwards, on the way home in the car, Thai said to me, somewhat enigmatically, 'You know, it wouldn't surprise me if you danced with Philip Banyer at some stage in your life.'

I just laughed: 'Don't be daft: Philip Banyer's way out of my league.' He was about to win the British Ballroom Dance Championships and bound for glory. Thai's comments seemed insane, and I thought they were probably born more of his own insecurity than any accurate estimation of my talents at the time.

But there was a grain of truth hidden somewhere in what he said. I had outgrown him, and although we still danced together for quite a while after that, I was increasingly aware that I needed to move on. I felt stuck, participating in low-level competitions, and I wanted to aim higher. Fortunately for both of us, this growing realisation came at the point at which Thai had to move back to America with his job. It meant I didn't have to say anything and we could remain good friends with no trace of any bitterness.

I met Ko Barclay on the dance circuit and he, like Thai, was initially better than I was. But our progress was not as fast as I would have liked, and I was beginning to despair of ever finding the right person with whom to launch myself into the world of amateur dance championships. At this point I got word from Thai to ring Philip Banyer. He and his partner Michelle had just won the Closed British Ballroom Dancing Championships at the Winter Gardens in Blackpool. I was intrigued, so did as instructed. We chatted for ages and ages, the upshot being that Philip offered to give me private lessons to help me improve my technique with a view to a possible partnership with him. I could hardly believe my luck.

By now I had moved out of my flat in Queen's Park and into hospital accommodation at St Peter's in Chertsey where, after my trip to Guatemala and Mexico, I had started work as a Senior House Officer in Orthopaedics. This unit specialises in the management of fracture non-union (broken bones that do not heal). In addition to my work on the wards and in theatre, I took part in fracture and orthopaedic clinics. Once a week I acted as plaster technician, building Plaster of Paris casts around various bits of the body. One of the other advantages of working there was the big sports hall that was part of the hospital complex. It was here that Philip gave me lessons over a period of about a month. Four weeks of getting to know each other, and it became clear to me that he had decided he was going to train me to be his partner. More than anything in the world he wanted to get into professional, world-standard dance and start winning international cham-pionships. It was all very *Strictly Ballroom*, and I was essentially still a novice, but he was going to take me on. He was going to train me till I reached his standard and I could partner him in his ambition. I was his fair lady, and he was my Professor Higgins. Or so I thought. In the end, it turned out to be not quite *Pygmalion*.

The way Philip looked at it, his dance partner had to be his girlfriend. In his mind it was all or nothing, given that you spend your entire time together. I would have been happy just to date him, but that would have then been difficult, because he would have had to find himself another dance partner, and then he would have been out dancing with her all the time and have no time for us. It could not work any other way. The fact was that I shared his ambition anyway. I wanted to become a professional dancer more than anything else, so if my relationship with Philip appears to spring from an ulterior motive, then maybe it did. But if that was the case it was a motive that tapped into an unfulfilled childhood ambition, an all-consuming passion that continued to rule me. The desire to dance and dance at the highest level would not go away. It was something that I still craved, even after all those years. An opportunity had presented itself that might assist me to fulfil an old promise. It was an offer I could not refuse.

It was at this point that the dancing and the doctoring finally collided and the collision was head-on. It was only a matter of time before one or the other was a casualty of the union, a casualty that no one in the Chertsey Orthopaedics unit would be able to fix. After a bit of plotting and planning I decided that it would be best for me to give up my career in medicine and focus instead on dancing. I had wanted it for years and I finally decided to try and build the potential for a new career in ballroom. I was to move in with Philip, into the flat where he lived above his parents in their house in Enfield. I would look for a hospital job that was Monday to Friday, nine to five, to give me an income and make time for rehearsals: every evening and practically every weekend. It would have to be a job that would take me off the medical career ladder, but allow me to earn my living as a doctor until I was ready to launch myself into life as a professional dancer.

6 Strictly Ballroom

EVERY NIGHT I USED TO practise. Every weekend I used to practise. Unless I got one basic step exactly right Philip would not let me progress to another. I did the first one, the featherstep from the foxtrot. It comprises about six strides, and until I managed to get that bit absolutely perfect I was not allowed to go any further. When you are doing this seven days a week for maybe three hours at a time it is totally soul destroying. But I was as determined as he was to succeed. I could be as stubborn as anyone.

Philip was not a Latin dancer, so I had taken a calculated risk and gambled on ballroom. I was probably better at Latin, but I saw the shift as a challenge and I wanted to make dance my profession. Destiny having denied me this opportunity the first time round, I felt as if fate had intervened to give me another chance. Where time and circumstance had conspired against me before, the road was clear now. That's how I looked at it anyway. I had a lot invested in my decision.

I found a non-career job that was not going to progress very far but gave me every evening and every weekend free. I became a Staff Grade physician in A&E at Chase Farm Hospital, Enfield. I moved in with Philip, who lived near by, and when I did so I took on his whole family, who were lovely people and very close knit. Philip's mother was a keen

competitive ballroom dancer. When she dressed to go dancing she looked fabulous: brightly coloured eye make-up,
sequins accentuating her profile and her hair always dressed
in elaborate styles, not a single strand out of place.

Philip was a plumber by trade. It was odd to see him change
from boiler fitter to ballroom dancer, but then I was a doctor
turned dancer, so neither of us fitted any particular stereo-
type. Like Thai before him he was another of my partners who
did not look typically ballroom. For a start he was too short,
but that obviously suited me. Even then he was a little too tall
for me, which caused some problems, though nothing that
either of us considered insurmountable. Certainly nothing so
mundane as my partner's height was going to get in my way. I
had given up my career in medicine to dance with him.

When I first saw Philip dance in Southall I was very
impressed. Despite Thai's prediction, it had never occurred to
me that one day I would partner him. So the situation in
which I now found myself felt like a dream come true. The
respect in which I held him as a dancer deepened into
something more when he started to give me lessons. He
obviously thought that I had potential, but not only that:
because I was a ballet dancer by training, I had the posture
and looks that went with it. Philip felt he could train me
quickly to a professional standard. This was the nub of the
conversation he had had with Thai. About to split with his
existing dance partner, he considered me a possible replace-
ment. But, apart from anything else, he liked me a lot too.

Philip was very encouraging in the beginning, he used to
play me the song 'For as long as it takes I will wait for you'.
But gradually, as the months rolled by (and in his view I was
still not getting the hang of it) he would throw his arms in the
air and say: 'I can't dance with you.'

There was a blockage. I was blocked by then and, though
I might understand his frustration, this was not the way to
bring out the best in me. We did that same step for the next
six months.

I got more and more miserable. Very occasionally we would do a bit more, but most of the time it was just this one step. Philip was as obsessive about his dancing as I had been about my doctoring. It did not exactly complement the other aspects of his life and he was sure about one thing: he did not want to be a plumber forever. He wanted a career in dance, and the only way to get one that was both fulfilling and yielded decent money was to become a world champion, or at the very least get close to it.

Philip's aim was to be world champion and he would accept no substitute. He was getting older – actually by then only a year older than I was – but he felt he was running out of time. His was an ambition made harder by his stubborn determination to triumph over all the odds and make a silk purse out of me. At that stage I was very much a sow's ear in the league of ballroom dancing. A lot of Philip's teachers had told him that you can't take a girl who is so far below you in ability and get her to the same level quickly. He was therefore going against all the advice but he felt I was the right dancer for him, and he wanted to prove everybody wrong. But it really wasn't working.

Together with the feather step was the equally insurmountable obstacle of 'Taking Up Hold'. When you walk on to the floor and prepare to dance you get yourself into a position whereby the man stands with his arms out ready to receive his female partner. Philip would stand thus, positioning me at a distance of some twenty-five feet away from him. I was not allowed to look him in the eye as I walked towards him, to slot myself into his embrace. If you are simply practising you can start dancing without all that rigmarole, especially as all he had planned were the first six strides of the first step of the foxtrot. But Philip was a stickler for perfection and that is how we practised. After a while, though, I no longer felt like walking in stiffly with my nose in the air and I started to act up. I dealt with the stress by being silly. When Philip asked me to lean a bit more to the right, I would lean over massively, exaggerating the movement. I had just got to the stage where I was so wound up that I couldn't do it. I could not even try to do it. It was all a mess.

On the face of it the dancing was going badly, but actually it was not all misery. I was improving my own technique considerably, because we were travelling round the country for lessons with some of the most respected dancers in the field: Amersham to work with Michael and Vicki Barr; Richard and Janet Gleave in Kingston; Fay and Anthony Hurley in Guildford – all of whom were world champions in their time and all of whom gave me endless encouragement. We would drive down for the day, have our lesson and drive back again. We usually did this a couple of times a week and I loved those lessons.

I was also learning to teach ballroom dancing. Philip wanted to teach because it was part of turning professional, so I had to learn too. One of the bibles of ballroom, Alex Moore's *The Revised Technique of Ballroom Dancing* (first published in 1948, into its ninth edition and reprinting 30 years later) was a book I studied. Moore, a fellow and examiner of the Imperial Society of Teachers of Dancing, ran the Zeeta Dance Studios in Kingston upon Thames, and his Monthly Letter Service, or MLS as it was fondly known, was billed as having helped thousands of students and teachers throughout the world. Moore may well have helped the multitude since 1933 but I found it impenetrable. The only thing I learned from this and the myriad other tomes on ballroom technique, was that it is one thing knowing how to do dance but quite another knowing how to describe it for an exam. Right foot three-quarters of an inch to the left, head turned two-thirds of a shoulder turn and so on. It's complicated. And you don't actually need it. I didn't take any exams in the end, though I shall get round to them some day. They are still on my list of 'Things to Do'.

Philip and I never did reach the stage of dancing competitively together. When we went for lessons with the Gleaves and the Barrs I would do a little bit more each time, and they would dance with me. Then they would put the two of us together, always with the same outcome. They would ask Philip what he felt I was doing wrong. He would tell them in no uncertain terms, and then they would dance with me to see if they felt that was so. Sometimes they would say it was this and other times that, and we would try and adjust it accordingly. I didn't have much of a problem dancing with the teachers, mainly because I was more relaxed with them. As soon as you tense, you can't dance because you lose the freedom to move. I think I was so stressed generally that I couldn't dance with Philip any more, but when I danced with the teachers it was fine. A couple of them were encouraging: 'She's getting very good. Why can't you dance with her?'

Philip was still way better than I was, but most things are compromise and to a certain extent he needed to adjust his dancing to fit me. But he was unwilling to do that. He needed to become a bit smaller, so he needed to drop his body to fit me. Because he was small anyway he was not going to release the tightly held posture that he had. He could have made it work, but he did not want to: he did not want to adapt, to be the one to adjust.

To cap it all Philip then decided that I had the wrong image for ballroom dancing. As a ballet dancer you practise in tracksuit trousers and leotard, in anything in which you can move comfortably. You get hot, and you get sweaty, so you scrape your hair back in a bun. This isn't the ballroom way. When you go to practise you have to dress up. You have to wear a frothy skirt and a blouse; you apply full make-up and put up your hair. I couldn't see the point of this. I think I failed to realise that this was the way of life to which Philip had been raised so it was something he expected. His mother was still doing senior competitions, and competitive dancing was all he had known since he was a child. She had taken him to ballroom-dancing classes when he was very young, and he knew every twist and turn of that world. It fitted him like a glove, but I was a fish out of water. There was a language to ballroom culture that I could not deconstruct – nor, in truth, did I wish to.

Philip wanted me to go blonde. He felt that would be good for the image he had in mind for us. I already have blondish hair, but he wanted peroxide – white blonde, Monroesque, and I would not do it. My refusal became a major issue between us. He was so immersed in ballroom and getting it right that he would try anything to succeed. He even used spray-on hair, aptly named 'Mane', because he was going thin on top. When I saw him at a competition a few years after we had given up on our attempt to make it as dance partners I noticed he was wearing a toupee. The fact was, although Philip was emotionally involved with me, his main relationship was with ballroom. How he felt about me was inextricably linked with that, his first passion. To begin with our passions had coincided. Now they collided.

On outings to watch competitions, something we did quite frequently so as to learn and absorb new ideas, he preferred I dress à la ballroom. Glittery tops, full skirts and heels were de rigueur, as well as the over-bright make-up. Once again we didn't see eye to eye. I didn't see why I should dress up. Why could I not just wear a pair of trousers and a T-shirt and dress casually if I felt comfortable like that? Of course it was not just Philip's whim. There was peer-group pressure: everybody else in those circles conformed. I did not see why I should, but though I did not buy into it, occasionally I gave in.

However, Philip was adamant that my non-conformist attitude meant that I was not putting everything into our dancing. In his mind my reluctance to look the part at every opportunity manifested a weakness in my will to succeed. I suppose I could have become a peroxide blonde, but that presented me with a problem. While I was not yet a professional dancer, I still had a profession. I was still a doctor. I still had to go into work and look like a doctor. I guess that because the dancing wasn't going well I was losing sight of a future in it. I could not see myself becoming a full-time dance teacher either, so I didn't want to put my medical career in jeopardy. Medicine was important, not least because if all this failed I would still have a job, a means of earning a living. Conflicting ideas, conflicting desires and opinions: it was all leading inexorably to one final destination – pistols at dawn.

The shoot-out came in a practice class in Putney, southwest London. Halfway through, right in front of everybody, Philip stopped mid-step, flung his arms in the air and announced that he couldn't dance with me. He walked off the floor. I burst into tears and dashed out in the opposite direction. That was often how it was, but I had reached the end of my tether and I knew it. This time it really was it. Equally, I knew it from Philip's tone, and we were over and done with. It was a cold February day in 1996. I had been dancing with Philip for twelve months. That night I left the flat in Enfield for good.

I had nowhere to go. My own flat in Queen's Park was rented, so I had no home of my own to flee to. With my family the only option, Philip's father kindly drove my cats and me to Paddington Station to catch the train to Bristol that same evening. And so my world fell apart.

Fortunately my family, especially my mother, were there to help me pick up the pieces. My hospital employers, Chase Farm, proved stalwart, giving me a couple of weeks' compassionate leave to sort myself out. It was just as well, because I wasn't in a fit state to do anything. I had given up everything to dance with Philip, and the gamble had failed. It had all fallen to pieces.

When I think back on it now I'm surprised I put up with so much for so long. I'm a strong person, perfectly able to stand up for myself. But when Philip had wanted to take me on I had felt overwhelmed by the compliment. It was the challenge that I had been waiting for since I had turned down that place at the Royal Ballet School. I had wanted to make it as a dancer then, and the passing of the years had in no way diminished this desire. In fact they had done the opposite. The one thing you cannot have is the one thing you want, above all else. Dance was my Holy Grail. Taking that journey with Philip was part of my pilgrimage, my search for the part of myself that I had always experienced as missing. That must have been how it was, a kind of homage to that element of myself, my past unfulfilled. When I consider it in those terms I think it partly explains why I was so devastated when Philip washed his hands of me.

Within one week I discovered that Philip had lined up a new partner-cum-girlfriend. Subsequently they moved to Switzerland together, though later they too would split up. Apparently he has just married his current dance partner, and she is pregnant with their first child. I guess he must be happy now, because by all accounts he is earning a living from ballroom dancing.

I went back to work at the hospital and lived temporarily with my sister Julie, in Putney, commuting daily to Chase Farm. However, I didn't go back to the hospital with any renewed fire for medicine, I returned mostly for the want of something better to do. I still had to earn my living. There was a lot that was unresolved in my life. The split with Philip was so much more than losing my dance partner and the possibility of that illusive career. Just before we split I had said to him: 'OK, if you can't dance with me, so be it. Let's both get more suitable dance partners. But let's carry on going out together.'

But he was having none of that. And yet six months after our separation he came back to England for a few weeks and asked if we could meet up. We talked and then out of the blue he asked me to marry him. I was shocked. Maybe I should have been flattered, I don't really know. But I had been hurt very badly, rejected both personally and professionally: after that marriage was never even an option.

My mother had not encouraged me to change my mind. She had never liked Philip. She said that he was not seeing me for who I was but trying to mould me into a plastic imitation of what he wanted for himself. She may have been right, but I think she disliked him most because I was such a mess afterwards. I can understand why he behaved as he did; he was only doing what he saw as his job and I knew how important ballroom was to him. Outside of the dancing, when we were not practising, or watching dance videos or going to dance competitions (which was virtually non-stop) he was very nice to me. But I should have recognised the warning signs. I should have known better the day we went to see *Strictly Ballroom*, and he failed to see the funny side of it. He thought the film would be really good for the image of ballroom dancing. He was so immersed in that world that he could not see it for what it is. There was no sense of perspective, even of irony. But maybe that is the point of compulsive and grand obsessions: perhaps it is only from them that great achievement comes.

After our split three of the couples to whom we had been going for lessons did something really surprising. Usually at that level of dance they would teach only couples, because dancing with an individual can spoil their own technique. They would dance individual steps with you, but most of the time they watch and work on improving your dancing as a couple. However, because they were so upset by everything that had gone on between Philip and myself, they told me that until I found another partner they were prepared to give me lessons on my own. I appreciated this gesture immensely. It's so easy to kick people when they are down. Their continued support was a blessing and got me back on my feet and dancing again in no time. It was an enormous encourage-ment and made me feel a whole lot better.

When I started lessons again I found that my dancing had come on by leaps and bounds, and that actually I was a good-enough dancer. Gradually I began to accept that just because Philip wasn't able to dance with me, it didn't mean no one else in the world couldn't either. To say this was helpful would be a massive understatement, because, quite understandably, my self-esteem had taken a nose-dive.

My next step was to find myself another partner. Andrew Devlin was introduced to me by one of my dance teachers. He was very small, and physically we matched perfectly. What was even better was that he was a fanatical Latin dancer and didn't particularly like ballroom. I had not done much Latin for a while and subsequently I was better at ballroom, so it worked out well, me helping him with his ballroom and vice versa. When we were good enough, we said, we would do some competitions. We practised and practised and when we *were* good enough that's exactly what we did.

My Latin came on a pace, and Andrew's ballroom improved by leaps and bounds. We made the Top Twenty for the UK in both dance forms, ranking within the top 48 in the world. I danced with Andrew for the best part of a year, by the end of which I had moved back into my flat in Queen's Park.

Dance was still important to me and I practised with Andrew in any free time I had. We would go to competitions in Blackpool, Bournemouth and even Southall. In Blackpool the big competitions are held at the Winter Gardens. In Bournemouth it was the International Centre. I did all this and I loved it. I got on well with Andrew, even though he could be temperamental and his timekeeping left a lot to be desired. I really enjoyed dancing with him. He used to laugh at me and say: 'Come on, you have to behave more seductively with me.'

It was difficult though, for me to flirt with him as we had no romantic inclinations whatsoever towards each other.

By this stage I had reached the level of competition at which hair and make-up were vitally important. I used to apply layers and layers of fake tan, make up my eyes, varnish my nails, the works. For a Latin competition in Southall I decided I would really push the boat out and buy a hair extension. I used to spray my hair to make it look darker, using something I could wash out afterwards. This time I scraped it all into a very tight bun on one side of my head and attached a beautiful curling hairpiece that tumbled down my side in a sumptuous cascade of ringlets. I wore an off the shoulder dress, long and velvet and black, edged with gold trim and hemmed with a feather boa. The skirt was slashed to reveal the leg to my upper thigh. It looked perfect, but it was a difficult dress to dance in because the boa was so heavy it would slap my legs as I swung round, threatening to trip me up. My strappy, high-heeled gold sandals did not help either. With glitter on my face and body make-up, it all combined to turn me into a shimmering exotic example of the archetypal Latin dancer.

Notwithstanding the fact that I couldn't dance in the dress, I did match the occasion which, in a word, was glitzy. The lighting in the ballroom was the only thing about it that was subdued, though even then, around the high arches of Victorian doors and windows, there were row upon row of coloured fairy lights. We soon got into the spirit of things and all was going well, fiery and fast, until out of the corner of my eye I spotted something airborne. During a spin it had flown by me. It looked like a dead rat. I saw it again as I spun round once more and caught sight of it landing with a plop in the middle of the parquet floor. The same floor could happily have opened and swallowed me up as I realised it was my hairpiece. There it was, lying there like a dead thing as we danced on past. I finished with a tight fat knot above my right ear, strands of hair designed only as a foundation piece. As we whirled and twirled towards our finale I heard Andrew's *sotto voce* comments, but I carried on regardless. When we had finished I walked off the floor, scooping my hairpiece up nonchalantly as I went. Video cameras were recording the event, and for years to come I worried that one day I would find myself the inadvertent victim of Jeremy Beadle and Co. on *You've Been Framed*.

Needless to say I never wore that hairpiece again, but I continued to dress to the nines, especially for one top-level ballroom-dancing competition Andrew and I entered in Hemel Hempstead. This was an International Championship, and I had a new dress made especially for it. Very pale pearly-pink satin with sleeve drapes of see-through chiffon, open from shoulder to wrist on one side and fixed at the cuff by an encrustation of creamy pearls. The low-cut bodice was also edged with pearls, but the icing was the tiers of boa round the bottom of the hem, like ridges of surf at the sea's edge, they just brushed clear of the floor. With high heels in colour-matched satin, I loved this outfit. It still hangs in my wardrobe, alongside the casual, sporty clothes I wear at home and the sober black trousers and tops for when I'm on duty at the hospital.

A year or so after we had first started to dance together Andrew and I were asked to appear on *Come Dancing*. Andrew, however, had decided by then that he wanted to stop for a while, a decision precipitated by an operation on his knee. When he recovered he decided that he no longer wanted to do ballroom but concentrate only on Latin. He needed to find himself a new and like-minded partner, because I had no desire to give up ballroom. Quite amicably, we agreed to go our separate ways.

A month or so went by and I had failed to find a new partner. I was beginning to feel downhearted again, and I did not know what to do with myself. I felt I had nothing to aim for. I had no plans, and I felt I had no future. The future I once had had as a doctor I had given up to dance with Philip.

7 Helicopter Emergency Medical Service

ALTHOUGH MY WORLD HAD SPUN OFF its axis somewhat after the harrowing interlude with Philip and the fall-out that followed, the experience had proved useful in a sense: it had served to exorcise a few ghosts, in particular my dream of becoming a professional dancer. Now my future in ballroom was all but washed up, I was keen to breathe fresh life into my medical career. Although it took time to find my way again, I was almost sure the path was leading me back to medicine. I was ready to see what I could make of my life as a doctor. It no longer felt like second best, but if medicine in general was now my goal, I needed to sort out what exact form that goal would take.

I had not given it up entirely while I had been dancing with Philip and Andrew. As a Staff Grade Physician at Chase Farm I was involved in teaching and supervising Senior House Officers, medical students and nursing staff. I also went on a couple of training courses, one in Advanced Trauma, the other in Cardiac Life Support.

While I was at Chase Farm I learned something that was not on any medical curriculum. The husband of one of my colleagues was having chest problems, and when he came in for an X-ray a shadow was found on his lung. During a return appointment, at the request of my colleague, I had a look at the new X-rays, but could find nothing. The shadowing had gone, as it sometimes does. I asked the radiologist for a second opinion, and he reached the same conclusion. Armed with this comforting information I walked into the waiting room.

He was fine, but he didn't know it then. I looked at him with a serious expression on my face, and then I told him: 'I'm sorry, you've only got a couple of days to live.'

For a second or so he stared at me, then his eyes rolled and he started to choke. Within seconds he was in the throes of a grand-mal epileptic fit. I'd been joking, but the joke had backfired, badly. We rushed him straight into A&E, and I was panicking.

He was slow to come round, and when he finally did it was obvious he had a weakness down one side of his body, one of the symptoms of a stroke. I was extremely worried, almost distraught, thinking that my few foolish words had triggered the attack, and that he might never fully recover. Both his wife and my boss tried to reassure me otherwise, but I just sat in the coffee room, miserable and terrified, berating and chastising myself.

It wasn't until almost a year later that I learned what happened to him. His collapse that day proved a watershed for him. He had been through a very frightening experience and when he did pull through, he decided to take drastic action. He therefore embraced a healthier lifestyle and once he had done that he didn't look back. Feeling happier and more resilient than he had in years, his health problems simply evaporated. In a way I did him a favour, though I'm not keen to repeat it. It taught me a lot too. I am much more careful about joking with my patients now.

Life is a series of lessons, some of which you learn from immediately, like the one I just described, others you have to be taught time and time again before you get the message. The proverbial brick wall syndrome. My own particular learning curve, certainly as far as my medical career was concerned, seemed to follow the second pattern, I suppose largely because I had never been clear in my own mind that medicine was for me. But now that I was so much more positive about it as a career choice, I started to look around for fresh opportunities and really consider my options.

The Helicopter Emergency Medical Service (HEMS) had captured my imagination ever since it was started in 1989, just after I had graduated from St Mary's. It was a result of the initiative of two doctors, A&E consultant Alastair Wilson and consultant surgeon Richard Earlham, both based at the Royal London in Whitechapel. It quickly gained a reputation within the medical fraternity as one of the most exciting and stressful jobs you could do.

Medical helicopters existed in other countries before London's HEMS, and their value was well documented. There were all sorts of studies around, one of which was an assessment by the Rotterdam HEMS in Holland. The statistics speak for themselves: the lives of between 10 and 15 per cent more people were saved as a result of the prompt treatment they received by a doctor flown by helicopter to treat them on scene; this rose to 25 per cent for those injured in road-traffic accidents. In Britain 16,000 people die each year because of trauma, or serious accidental injury, with about 25 per cent of these deaths a result of Road Traffic Accidents (RTAs). Using the Rotterdam percentages as a guideline, that would mean saving the lives of between 1,600 and 2,400 more people every year, with 1,000 more survivors of car accidents.

In London the helicopter serves over 10 million people, almost 20 per cent of the UK population, and every one of them can be reached within 15 minutes. Although statistically quite a small percentage, multiple trauma victims need the care of professionals who are working daily with trauma. Trauma is what HEMS does best partly because that's its remit. By definition it deals with trauma. Since inception it has built up a level of expertise that is unparalleled anywhere in the UK, dealing with in excess of 9,000 incidents since 1989. On average the service saves 30 lives a year, largely by taking A&E to the patient as opposed to the other way round. It is not just an air ambulance, it provides in-depth medical treatment at the scene of an accident.

A medical helicopter service had been a gap in the market that was waiting to be filled, but it took time, effort and persistence to get it up and running. Ultimately it was agreed that its doctors would come from the National Health Service and its paramedics from the London Ambulance Service (LAS), with its calls processed by Central Ambulance Control in Waterloo, where all the capital's 999 calls are processed and channelled.

Here, a HEMS Special Incident Desk would be manned by the helicopter paramedics. They would monitor the calls, filter out the ones that required its expertise and pass them on to the HEMS operations base. The final push, literally to get the new service off the ground, was made possible only with sponsorship of the helicopter by the Express Newspaper group, and by the early 1990s the canary-yellow helicopter had become a familiar sight in the skies above London.

I would see it from time to time, sometimes from the window of my flat, sometimes on my way to or from work. What appealed to me was how HEMS worked at the absolute cutting edge of Accident and Emergency medicine, pushing back the boundaries all the time. It was something I wanted to be involved with desperately, but to do so I had to brace myself for yet more exams in order to qualify. In A&E work, of which HEMS is just a part, there is the choice of specialising in medicine, surgery or anaesthetics. This is reflected in the qualifying exams. A&E will accept any of them. I steeled myself to do the medical ones and become a Member of the Royal College of Physicians (MRCP). These are dreaded exams for doctors. They are very difficult, but I had to pass them before I could even think of applying for HEMS or progressing on to become a consultant. Without membership of the Royal College of Physicians I would either have to stay at Staff Grade level or become a Clinical Assistant, because there was no career progress in a hospital without it. I could of course have switched lanes and tried for general practice, taking a different set of exams to qualify as a GP, but that did not fire me up. There was not enough excitement in it for me.

This new situation gave me a strong sense of *déjà vu*. I was acutely aware of the high price of not following a dream. I knew if I didn't try I would hanker after what might have been, which was no way to live my life. There was only one way to get what I wanted, hard work and single-minded dedication. But I felt good, I had decided on medicine and now I had my eye on exactly the speciality I wanted.

My life had reached a new and exciting fork in the road, and knowing where my long-term future would lie, I decided to take a break and go travelling for a year. Kenya, along with Central America, had whetted my appetite for foreign parts. I had nothing holding me back – no husband, no dance ambition, no job to which I was yet fully dedicated. I told myself that when I came back I would sit Part One of the MRCP. This was OK, the year out would give me time to think and get myself fully prepared for the rigours of more medical exams. But my boss at Chase Farm, Mr Mikhail, had other ideas. He agreed to give me a sabbatical, leave my job open for a year, but on one condition: he told me I had to take Part One of the MRCP *before* I left. If I didn't want to wander aimlessly, if I wanted a job and purpose to come back to, I had little choice but to sit the exam as he was insisting. With hindsight it was a good thing since he gave me the push I now know I desperately needed.

If I was actually bribed into doing it, it was a tactic that worked, because I studied like a fiend for the next few months. When D-Day dawned I took myself off to the examination centre in Euston, north London, feeling so nervous I thought I was going to be sick. On the way there I found myself sitting on the tube next to an elderly woman. She was in a fragile state of mind, because her husband had recently died, and she talked to me non-stop from Queen's Park to Euston Square, a journey eight stations long. People generally find me easy to talk to, and I tend to attract those who want someone to pour their hearts out to. She obviously needed to get things off her chest, but she did me a good turn too. It was almost as if she had been sent to take my mind off things, because by the time we got to Euston I was more worried about her than me. When we emerged from the Underground together, I walked her down the road, branching off when I got to the hall where I was to sit the exam. I bless her to this day.

I had calmed right down on the trip across London, but when I took my seat in the examination room my heart was in my mouth. I took a deep breath and when the papers were handed out, I quickly scanned the questions. Part One comprises a multiple-choice written paper, but it is negatively marked, so if you get an answer wrong you are marked minus one. The scope of the exam covers the minutiae of medicine, which to my view is fairly irrelevant for normal day-to-day practice. It is extremely difficult to encompass entirely, as reflected in the 30 per cent pass rate. There is not a mark by which you pass or fail; the examining board just takes the top 30 per cent and then draws a line, above which you pass, below which you fail. The pass mark varies, and the thinking behind this is that because so many people take it, the standard will always be constant at the 30 per cent cut-off. I had taken it three or four years earlier and failed by 0.5 of a per cent, having got 61 with a pass mark of 61.5. That had been a bitter pill to swallow and made me even more nervous of failure as I sat there a second time.

I glanced round that huge room, looking at the other entrants. They all seemed to have their heads down and be working steadily through the questions. That's the worst thing you can witness in an exam room, everyone steaming ahead when you're sitting there and panicking. You could have heard a pin drop, nothing but scratching pens to nibble at the silence. I caught the eye of someone a few rows distant, but they quickly looked away. I felt very alone and isolated, and right then, I wanted to be anywhere but where I was. I had looked at the paper and decided I could not answer anything accurately. Guessing was not an option, because if I did so incorrectly I would be marked down. I was in such a quandary I just sat there with the well of panic getting deeper and deeper inside me, totally negative and with one thought only going round and round my head: I don't stand a hope in hell.

In the end I did have a crack at it, for better or worse, what else could I do? But I walked out before the allotted time was up, and I had only answered just over 50 per cent of the questions. I was really depressed, terribly demoralised, because it is the toughest exam I was ever to take, and I had worked hard for it. Even more galling was the fact that failure would place a full stop against my medical ambitions. I had just surrendered my long-held hopes for a career as a dancer, and the prospect of my profession as a doctor foundering on the rocks of the MRCP was intolerably hard to face.

So I decided not to face it. It was early February when I took the exam, and I had purposefully booked my flight to Delhi for the fifteenth. That was a good few days before the MRCP results were released, and when I flew out of Heathrow, though I did not know the outcome for sure, I was convinced I had failed. There was nothing I could do now, so I consciously banished all thought of it from my mind and focused instead on the world that lay at my feet. I was about to travel round Southeast Asia. It would be the trip of a lifetime, and nobody and no thoughts of the future were going to spoil it for me.

But when you go away, you take yourself with you, and as reliably as ever my subconscious kicked in. The first two weeks or so in India I had bad dreams about the exams and their aftermath. There I was on a new continent, home to one of the oldest known civilisations in history, a place of enormous variety, vibrancy and colour, and I was back in that grim examination hall in north London. I would wake in a cold sweat after a nightmare, frozen with fear in front of a blank sheet of paper. Nothing was written and I could think of nothing, my mind as bare as the page on the desk before me. I would lie there and try to comfort myself with the thought that I had not passed anyway and there was nothing I could do about it, so there was nothing to fear. I should just enjoy my year off, and immerse myself in my travels, absorb all that India and the rest of Asia had to offer. That's fine in principle, but I was not an aimless wanderer. And that's what this felt like now. Instead of going back to the medical exams, with thoughts of HEMS and a future, I had nothing to go back to at all. I was distracted by the trip to some extent, but not enough. I knew I would have to face the music at the end of it. I had vowed to myself that I would not retake the exam when I returned to England. I was simply not going to go through the pain of all that study again, never mind the agony of the exam itself. I told myself I would continue with my staff-grade job, progress no further up the career ladder of medicine, and that would be the end of it. But I don't like settling for second best and I am not a good loser, so no matter where I went, what I saw or what I tried to experience, there was always the nagging worry at the back of my mind, What was I going to do with my life?

It was nearly three weeks before I phoned home to speak to my mother. I wanted to find out how she was and reassure her I was alive and well. I was in Jaisalmer, one of India's most exotic and unusual towns, a remote and medieval-looking place in Rajasthan. It looked like it had been plucked from the pages of the *Arabian Nights*. It was known as the golden city and today it is very much a living museum; centuries ago its strategic position on the camel-train routes between India and Central Asia brought it great wealth.

It was a very bad line, but I strained to hear news of my family, my mother's voice kept coming and going. I think I hadn't wanted to know anything other than that all was well back home and to reassure them I was fine. It was my mother, however, who brought up the subject of the dreaded exam.

'Don't you want to know the results?' she asked.

I already knew the outcome, I told her, so why ruin my year off completely?

'This time you might want me to tell you,' she persisted.

'Well, I don't, actually.'

'You do, Heather. You passed.'

What? Somebody run that by me again? I had completed little more than fifty per cent of the questions, left early and had nightmares ever since. I had been quite determined not to introduce any harsh reality into the exotic world that surrounded me, but this reality was wonderful. A little bit of irony in that: I hadn't really phoned for the results and yet in a way I had.

What I heard took me so much by surprise that I almost dropped the phone, so certain had I been that I was a failure and my trip would be tarnished until I returned home and did something about it. I thought of a city rich in trade and now there was I, suddenly rich in tidings, as wealthy as I have ever felt in my life. Through all the crackling and interference over the telephone line I heard enough to know that when I returned to London it would be to resume my *career* as a hospital doctor. Not job, career: I had achieved a mark that just fell on the right side of the pass-fail divide, something like 44.75% with the cut-off at 44.30.

I had just about scraped through, but that did not matter, any pass was good enough. I was suddenly ecstatic. I could not believe I had made it, but I went out to celebrate in style that night.

The next day I left on a four-day camel safari. I felt complete, vital and alive. It was good to have the sun on my face today: all was well with the world. Not even the extreme discomfort of riding a camel in the desert could dent my happiness. Rajasthan is known as the Land of Kings, and for a while over the next few days, cliché as it might be, I felt like its queen.

There was only one blot on the landscape, and it only occurred to me once the initial euphoria had worn off. I would have to take Part Two of the MRCP when I got back. But I could put that fear on ice for the moment and concentrate on the road ahead.

I travelled extensively for almost a year, throughout South-east Asia, part of it with a friend, whom I had met initially through salsa lessons. We both took the same class, and when I had told him I was going off to Asia, he expressed interest in coming with me. I don't mind travelling alone, but sometimes it's nice to have a companion. As it turned out he didn't enjoy travelling. He had left behind his four-year-old daughter in England, and as the months went by he missed her far more than he expected. He also didn't take to roughing it, backpacking and living on the cheap. Some people love travelling like that and some do not: he fell into the latter category. We parted company at half time, just as we were about to leave China. By then he was pretty miserable. If you are away with someone who is not enjoying it, it's no fun, and when I carried on alone to Burma and Indonesia, I was a lot happier. You are, of course, never on your own when you travel, and I was always meeting people and joining up with them for a few days of companionable backpacking. I made a lot of new friends that way, including a new boyfriend, Steve.

I left Indonesia and flew home in time for Christmas. Steve came with me. We were to live happily together for the next three years. That new year, 1996, I went back to Chase Farm, where my boss had proved as good as his word. He was like my guardian angel, having first cornered me with his ultimatum, then standing by me through a period of great uncertainty. Now I, like him, had no doubt that I would really make it as a consultant.

Life was more light hearted after my sabbatical, even with the knowledge that some time in the not-too-distant future I would have to take Part Two, the clinical stage of the MRCP. This was the practical side of the qualification process where, in addition to studying the books, I had to work with the patients. To give myself the best chance of success I took a secondment as a Senior House Officer (SHO) in Medicine at Chase Farm for six months, where I studied and studied the case notes of the patients I saw, building the practical experience I required. The work is diagnostic and involves picking up clinical signs in patients who are admitted to hospital, looking at ECGs and X-rays. I really enjoyed it. It was fun and very satisfying, especially when I got it right. The exam, which I took at Gloucester Hospital, was wonderful. I found it more like a quiz than the ordeal I had suffered in Euston.

My first case was a man with a very unusual heart murmur. A normal heartbeat is quite regular, *lub dub, lub dub, lub dub*. But what I had heard when I put my stethoscope to his chest was a beat like none I had come across before. I listened and I listened and as I did it gradually became more recognisable. Although it is considered by many to be something of an art form, there is actually nothing mystical about the interpretation of heart sounds. It does, however, require a basic understanding of the normal cardiac cycle, and why and where it can occasionally go wrong. It also demands practice and a trained ear. There are various ways of doing this, and I was lucky enough to find a really excellent one. It was a tip that I got from a consultant friend and involved the borrowing of a tape of heartbeats from a drug company. In between listening to soul and jazz on my stereo I would play my tape of heart sounds. The trick was to cover a speaker with a towel then crouch down beside it and listen via my stethoscope. It sounded as if I were in an A&E cubicle, doing a heart check on a patient. Unorthodox as it may sound, that was how I practised and it was about to pay off.

I was convinced that the patient I was assessing had a condition known as 'fixed splitting of the second sound', where there is literally a split in the second beat: *lub dub-dub*. I was 99 per cent sure this was what it was, so I put my hands behind my back authoritatively and looked the examiner straight in the eye. His face lit up as I announced my diagnosis and I knew I was right. I sailed through the rest of the exam, delighted with myself. It was easy and given my lack of experience it should not have been. But lack of experience had never stopped me before and I was happy to try the unorthodox even the eccentric if that's what it took. I had learned to think on my feet in Kenya and was never afraid of making decisions. I studied that way and it carried me through now.

After that first question I was full of confidence and assessed each situation from that standpoint. The chances were that if I had got that first patient wrong I might have steadily lost the plot and gone downhill, but I hadn't. I had got it right and pushed on from that springboard. I was almost certain I had passed when later, during my viva, they let me go early. If I had needed more marks to help me, they would have kept me there but they didn't.

But it was another two weeks before I was to know for sure, and with time comes doubt, no matter how certain you think you are. That fortnight turned out to be quite disturbing. Have I passed? What if I haven't? I can't believe I haven't.

The day we were due to get our results I invited some friends round for a Mexican meal. Cooking is not my strong point, but I enjoy entertaining and developed a liking for Mexican food while I was in Central America. That evening when everyone had assembled in my living room to raise a glass to success – or in some cases down a drink to drown failure – I had to admit that the letter containing my exam results had failed to arrive. I had been expecting it to turn up all day, because occasionally the post was erratic, but by the time I got back with the Corona beer from the off-licence around six, it was still not lying on the mat. I was on tenterhooks and by eight o'clock, egged on by my friends, I decided to phone the GPO sorting office to ask if I could go down and look for my missing letter. They were only too happy to oblige, though, as they pointed out, I would have to wade through a ten-foot pile of mail to do so. I was in the middle of an evening with friends and decided to leave it till the morning, when the proposed search proved unnecessary. Fortunately, the letter arrived in the first post. I knew I had passed as soon as I saw it lying there on the mat. Failure was a thin envelope and mine was bulging with success. I burst into floods of tears.

I thought this would be the last exam I would ever have to take in my life, but things rarely work out quite as you expect. Although I didn't know it then, two more major exams lay ahead of me: my MSc in Sports Medicine, plus the new exit exam for doctors who work in A&E, the FFAEM (Fellowship of the Faculty of Accident and Emergency Medicine), which has been introduced since I passed my MRCP. It's a necessary qualification in order to become a consultant. To achieve this I shall need to do another year in an Accident and Emergency department. The FFAEM will gain me my Certificate of Completion of Specialist Training, and then I shall be able to apply for a consultant post somewhere. It is a long hard slog, but all part of the new set of guidelines for training A&E doctors, which had not existed before. Although it means a lot more work for me, it is a good development, because it ensures core knowledge of general medicine, general surgery, anaesthetics, orthopaedics and paediatrics. It is an important milestone and costs a small fortune to sit, about £700, but when the time comes I'll just have to bite the bullet.

For the moment, though, I could rest on my laurels, for with membership of the Royal College of Physicians under my belt the way was clear for me to move my career plan into a higher gear. I took up my first position as a Specialist

Registrar (SpR) in A&E in the Northwest Thames Rotation, and this was what I did for the next two and half years. Much more crucially, I had achieved the initial goal I set down after shelving my dancing career. I was now sufficiently qualified to consider putting in an application for a secondment to the Helicopter Emergency Medical Service.

When first I discussed my desire to make a stint with HEMS part of my A&E career path, I encountered some hostility within the profession. It became clear to me that certain people (who were not connected with HEMS) were resentful of it. There are a variety of views on how best to deal with trauma, accidental injuries, the shock of which may have long-lasting damage to health and well-being, and this has led to differing opinions of the value of the helicopter service. Maybe it is professional jealousy, perhaps simple ignorance of what the service does, but HEMS has not been without its detractors.

By the time I was eligible to apply, luckily I was working for a hospital that was not one of those against it, so I had their full support. I was delighted when eventually I got called for interview. On the appointed day, I arrived slightly early at the Royal London Hospital and sat waiting in a front office, chatting to the secretary and enjoying a laugh. A few people wandered in and out of reception in the course of the fifteen minutes I was ensconced there, including a casually dressed young man. We exchanged a little banter, before he wandered off along the corridor. I assumed he was one of the registrars, helping out with the interview procedure. I could not have been more wrong. The next time I saw him was behind the desk in the interview room. I had been sharing a jokey five minutes with Gareth Davies, consultant for the service. I tried to look relaxed yet professional, but I just wanted the earth to open up and swallow me. Here we go again, I thought. That's it: he's bound to think I'm too frivolous, too silly to fly round London answering emergencies in a helicopter. There's no way I'll get this job now!

8 A Matter of Life and Death

I WAS WRONG, AGAIN. MAYBE I SHOULD have more confidence in my ability because I always seem to expect and fear the worst. Yet I do have confidence, just not always at the time, at least as far as interviews or exams go. I'm fine in what I call real situations. Anyway, whatever: I was wrong. I did get the job with HEMS, only when the letter of acceptance came it was not quite what I had expected. I had been given notice to start, which was great. I had the job, only the start date was for eighteen months hence. Could I really wait that long?

It was October 1997 and it seemed so distant that I thought it would never actually materialise, one of those false promises like 'the cheque's in the post'. I knew that HEMS was at risk of closure due to lack of funding, so I worried away the next year and half, wondering what I would do if it folded before I had my chance.

As usual I need not have upset myself because HEMS was on a much firmer financial footing than it had been in a long time, and without wishing to tempt fate I understand it remains so today, partly because its true worth is at last beginning to be appreciated. It costs the London Ambulance Service (LAS) £250,000 a year to run one road ambulance with the annual running costs of the entire service reaching

£106 million. HEMS, at £1.2 million a year, is the equivalent of four land ambulances which, in the scheme of things, is nothing. Considering how much the whole of the London Ambulance Service costs, then HEMS is only a fraction of it. But a direct financial comparison is impossible when you consider the area HEMS covers, when you bear in mind its speed of response and what this means for an injured person, someone run over by a bus or pulled from a fire with first-degree burns, for example.

The helicopter works out at 12p per person per year, which at less than half the cost of a first-class stamp seems to me to be excellent value for money. There are other purely financial advantages of treating an injured patient quickly. It can cost as much as £1 million to look after just one patient with severe brain damage. This is someone who might not have ended up in such a bad way if HEMS had managed to get to them within that first crucial hour after the accident. By reducing the number of people who need lengthy after-care HEMS not only promises a better quality of life but can also save the NHS money in the long run.

When I heard I had been accepted, I also learned that a friend who had applied at the same time as me had not been accepted. She had been as desperately keen to join as I was but only one of us got the job. That numbed the excitement for me a little, because she was equally qualified and has similar attributes. Life has never been fair, however: it's random and arbitrary in nature. I had learned that lesson long ago. I felt for my friend because I could understand her disappointment, and I considered myself fortunate.

I have a penchant for the risky and dangerous. This is well known among my colleagues, but they also know that when the wheel comes off I do not lose my nerve. On my trip to Central America, I spent a night in Guatemala on the rim of a live volcano. I had gone there against the advice of everyone from the local tour guides to the Foreign Office. It was considered dangerous, not only because of volcanic activity but also the local mafia, who were targeting tourists. I decided that the chances of the volcano erupting were slim and so were the chances of being mugged or kidnapped, raped or murdered. So I took a calculated risk. I'm glad I did. It was awe inspiring and beautiful, sparks from molten lava lighting up the sky until dawn. The volcano looked as if it was on fire, a constant shower of white and yellow and red flame against the perfect black of the night: and yet the place had an extraordinary sense of peace and tranquillity about it. I enjoyed the thrill of learning to trust my instincts. The memory of that night will stay with me for the rest of my life. I made my decision and went with it: neither fear nor anxiety spoiled anything for me.

I am at my best in a crisis, situations where someone else might panic. The day Robin drove the 4WD into a ditch in the middle of the Kenyan game reserve I was scared of course. But the fear was not so overpowering that I lost my ability to reason, to think my way through that 24 hours we were marooned among the lions. The only thing that really gets to me mentally, really pulls out my negative thought processes is exams – apart from that I think I'm pretty unflappable.

That side of my nature was not tested in the eighteen months following the letter of acceptance. I remained hospital-bound as a Specialist Registrar in A&E with the Northwest Thames Rotation. I enjoyed the work, but towards Easter 1999 I was invited over to Whitechapel to find an orange flying suit to fit me. That was wonderful: my first taste of what was to come. It was real after all, HEMS wasn't closing down and the letter offering me a job had been telling the truth, the months were passing and the start date getting closer.

The flying suit was the HEMS doctors' uniform and finding one in my size proved a major headache. All of them were huge. They are a vital piece of kit with their 20 seconds of fire resistance, crucial for the job, and I had to have one. It had a long list of specifications, such as kneepads, which are very important because you spend all your time on them, and lots of pockets, to accommodate all the bits and pieces of medical equipment, mobile phones and suchlike you secrete in them. But it is not all good, there are drawbacks – for example, no warmth to the suit so you freeze in winter, but in summer it's too hot, and you sweat buckets. I learned to wear a tracksuit or thermals underneath when it was cold and just a T-shirt when it was warm. Another minus point was the material that it's made from: it is resistant to neither blood nor water, so you get soaked and stained in one way or another. It's made like that for good reason though, as any such fabric would be intolerably hot to wear. The suits are also extremely heavy when filled with kit, mine weighing in at around half a stone. My Thomas pack, the vital medical supplies bag that all HEMS doctors carry on their backs to the scene of an accident – weighed around another forty pounds on top.

Our footwear was hardly lightweight either – steel-capped boots, essential to protect our toes, and fundamental again because we kneel a lot on scene. The boots have special non-slip soles like those worn by oil-rig workers on North Sea drilling platforms. I am a size three and a half, and they do not make workmen's shoes in my size, so at the same time as ordering a suit to fit, I had some boots made specially for me.

My time finally came round and the night before I was due to start I could hardly sleep I felt so excited. I got up early in the morning and rode to my new job on my moped. That day is imprinted in my memory for all sorts of reasons, not least when a pigeon flew into me as I was driving through Maida Vale. It dropped, stunned, and I presume dead, into the gutter, though I did not stop to find out because I could not be late on my first day. As it was I arrived on the helipad feeling slightly traumatised: it may not sound much to a non-motorcyclist, but a pigeon is big and heavy enough to knock you off balance, not a good thing on two motorised wheels.

I talked about it over coffee and one of the pilots joked that next time I should pick up the bird and bring it in to roast on the barbecue they had built next to the helipad. Apparently this was the normal procedure whenever anything feathery got caught in the rotor blades of the helicopter, something that often happened when they landed on or near Trafalgar Square. Like a good vegetarian I blanked the pilot but, amusing as it might appear, it was a bizarrely apt induction to the job.

HEMS only takes doctors in the fourth year of their Specialist Registrar (SpR) training, just before we are due for a consultant's post. They don't want anyone who has not achieved that level of seniority. On average a HEMS doctor sees between 150 and 200 patients in the six months of their attachment. The secondment used to run for nine months, but they cut it back to six. The thinking was that by the end of six months any doctor would have contributed as much as he or she could, and would have seen and done most of what there is to see and do in that kind of service. Also, more doctors need to be given the chance to gain that experience.

There is no doubt that going out to badly injured, traumatised patients, making critical decisions that are invariably questioned and criticised when you get the patient back to the hospital, can be very stressful over a prolonged period. I was to be with HEMS from April through September.

What HEMS needs are doctors who are good in a crisis, doctors good in a team environment. Anybody can do the medicine: that bit is easy, at least it is if you are trained to SpR level. But handling serious trauma cases on scene is anything but easy, and no amount of training can help with the myriad emotions. Nor does it teach you how to work alongside the ambulance and fire crews, the police, as well as the media and any bystanders who might be trying to see what's happening and getting in the way. Knowing how to behave within the crisis is crucial. It was something that was drummed into us from Day One and we ignored it at our peril.

HEMS fell into disfavour with some of the other emergency services quite early on in its life. Apparently some of the team grew too big for their boots. Maybe the fact that they appeared out of the skies wearing bright-orange suits on a mission to save lives had nurtured delusions of grandeur. That distinctive and somewhat flamboyant image can work against the service, especially when the media build it up into something akin to *Top Gun*. There were stories of arrogant doctors punching paramedics, of medical heroics that included unnecessary treatments, such as being too ready to give a general anaesthetic. It may well be hearsay, because no one has ever come up with any concrete evidence, but word travelled fast on the hospital grapevine and, as with Chinese Whispers, the word became distorted. Pretty soon everyone in the service was tarred with the same brush, and it took a number of years to shake that image off.

Nowadays no one arrives on scene like Superman. I was to learn that HEMS is there to help, not take over, and of course this makes perfect sense. The last thing I wanted was to burst on scene and push someone already attending out of the way. As I discovered, the ground-ambulance crews do a fantastic job, and they can deal with almost anything.

One of the doctors I met during my first week was George Little. He was brilliant when on scene with other professionals, and he quickly became a role model for me. He was the author of a lot of my training, and he was the person I most admired and desired to imitate. I was not the only member of his fan club. Everybody loved George. When he left to become an A&E consultant at King's he presented me with Paddy, a little furry hedgehog badge with a shamrock – George is Irish – which often appeared later on press photos of me. He gave it to me as my good-luck mascot and, although not medically proven, I am convinced it works.

When I first accompanied George to the scene of an accident I noticed how he would crack a joke maybe, say or do something to put people at their ease. He believed that once the other services saw that he was a perfectly normal, down-to-earth person, not an arrogant fly-boy dropping out of the sky, then all the resentment melted away. He made it clear that he was as uncertain as the next person about what might happen next, and it was amazing how that refocused everyone's attention on the patient. He liked to formulate a plan of action that involved everyone. Everybody had a role to play, a function. As a result, a team was immediately formed and any lingering hostility fizzled out. When I talked to the crews afterwards, I would hear them tell us they were pleased we were there. They could have done X, but not Y. Y was what the patient needed. My experience of working with the ground crews is good; it is rare now for crews to be openly hostile. In fact many of them want to join HEMS.

Sean Clarke was a paramedic I was to work with a lot during my six months on the helipad, and one of the other members of the team I met during that first week. Based at Kenton Ambulance Station in Wembley, Sean was very pro-HEMS and had been keen for a secondment. Apparently he was not alone among his fellow paramedics. But while the waiting list of paramedics who want to join is long, it is also extremely tough to get in. HEMS holds a twofold attraction. The flying is a huge draw, but the serious multiple trauma and the opportunity to learn medicine fast and furiously working alongside doctors is unbeatable work experience. The number of trauma cases that a paramedic goes to on HEMS far exceeds anything they would encounter working on the ground ambulances. On average a road crew attends no more than two major trauma cases a year.

Doctors and paramedics working in tandem on HEMS make the best possible team. Obviously the ground-ambulance crews have a huge amount of experience on the street because that is where they are based, whereas doctors largely work in the fixed landscape of the hospital. A&E doctors function in a contained and ordered environment within four walls, but the road crews are on scene from the start of their career.

I find paramedics an interesting group, especially when you remember that to work on an ambulance all they need, qualification-wise, is a clean driving licence. No O Levels, no A Levels, nothing: it's amazing, considering the job they do, at the sharp end of A&E medicine. Certainly for my first month on HEMS and especially when I was out on my own, the paramedics used to hold my hand and get me through it. There are only certain things they are allowed to do however – it is all strictly controlled. They're probably able to do more interventional procedures than a nurse, even though they have much less training. Paramedics are very experienced at extrication, which is crucial for HEMS, because they attend a lot of road-traffic accidents and One-Under train casualties. In the course of their working life, paramedics encounter many more of these type of incidents than the average doctor does, so on scene their views matter.

The other member of the HEMS team to which I was officially presented was the one that sat in glorious isolation on the helipad. I could hardly wait to be introduced to the wonders of the helicopter, and I was shown around it that first morning by one of the firecrew, Paul Smith. He also took me through helipad and aircraft safety. The helicopter was built in 1982 in France, originally by Sud Aviation, which then became Aérospatial and is now part of EuroCopter. It is actually an SA365N Dauphin, and because of its age, although some of the parts are new, it is getting a bit raggedy round the edges and requires a lot of maintenance back at the Denham depot in Buckinghamshire. The aircraft is provided by Virgin, who took over the sponsorship from Express Newspapers in 1997. The M25 motorway is the rough boundary for its zone of operations, and the outlying county ambulances also occasionally call on its services. In the early days it attended the call outs from Denham and later Biggin Hill, until the helipad on the rooftop of the Royal London Hospital in Whitechapel was completed in August 1990. It now flies daily to the hospital from Denham, where it is hangared and kept up to scratch by a team of maintenance engineers.

Left Me with my younger sister Claire, at the Bristol Eistedfodd, 1979

Right Dancing in a display with my older sister Julie, 1970

As Ariel in *The Tempest*, 1977

As Peter Pan, 1980

Rag Week 1983: Me, Ann, Gail and Valentina at the pyjama party at Paddington station

Kinango Hospital

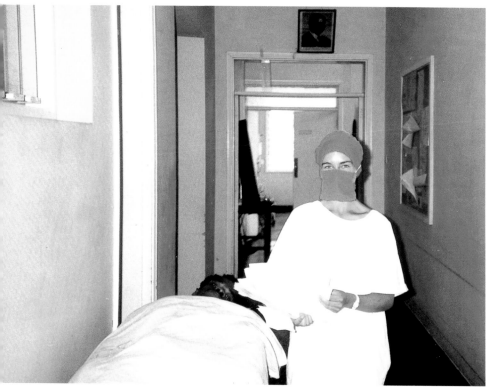

The unsuspecting patient goes to theatre!

Above Our luxurious apartment in Kinango!

Right The bats in the roof of our room

Below Lost up Mount Kenya with Robin

Left Andrew and I ballroom dancing at the International Championship in Hemel Hempstead, 1994

Right Andrew and I (wearing the rogue hairpiece!) at a Latin competition in Southall, 1993

Left The topsy-turvy life at HEMS!

Below The HEMS team, May 1999

Me with Steven Niland

It has a tendency to be temperamental and goes wrong too regularly. During my final month on HEMS it was totally out of commission because of a cracked rotor blade. The blades are always flexing, and one of them had a small crack in it, so it was sent off for repair. It came back just before the Paddington rail crash in September 1999, and they had a mass of engineers crawling all over it the morning of the crash, trying to get it back on line. There was no pressure on them to do that, but the engineers at Air Hanson feel part of the HEMS team, and they pulled out all the stops to get it fixed. But it was a long-winded procedure that involved tracking to stop vibrations and balancing all the blades so they fly on the same plane. Unfortunately it was too tricky to rush through to be of any help at Paddington, although Gareth Davies was the first doctor on scene that morning, and went on to oversee the lengthy medical evacuation.

Fortunately, courtesy of Virgin, the helicopter has now been replaced by something more modern and much quieter. As it is, it is too noisy to fly missions at night, something that it does not do in any case yet because of the safety implications. It is fully equipped as a medical helicopter.

Inside at the front there are the controls and seats for the captain and co-pilot. Towards the back there is a bed for the patient, at the head of which sits the doctor, with adjacent seats for the paramedic and an observer. We carry some equipment for us, for example our bright yellow helmets, vital protection when we have to crawl under tube trains or into tunnels or lift shafts, but most of the space is taken up with medical equipment for the patient. Fitted into the aircraft is piped oxygen, a ventilator and a 'helidyne' (the ratcheted trolley bed to get patients in and out of the helicopter. We also carry the Thomas pack, a fluid pack (containing three litres of warmed saline for intravenous infusion) and a Propaq to monitor pulse, blood pressure and ECG.

In the boot is one piece of equipment I never used – the MAST suit – an inflatable suit used in severe limb and pelvic injuries, which looks like something out of a sci-fi movie. By applying a tourniquet effect to the limbs and pelvis it helps to maintain a blood supply to the vital organs of the body. A&E hate it because you have to deflate it slowly over at least four hours, which keeps the patient in the department for too long. However, releasing it more quickly can cause a massive drop in blood pressure with the potential to kill the patient. With pelvic fractures there is also the potential for massive internal bleeding, so in less severe cases we used a pelvic splint – essentially an elastic corset that holds the pelvis together, thus stemming the bleeding. Similarly, with fractured femurs we use a Sagar splint, which pulls the leg straight by fitting into the groin and stretching the leg out. This holds the two ends of the bone together, again slowing the bleeding, but also reducing the pain. Alongside the splints we keep the thoracotomy kit.

Put simply, a thoracotomy is a surgical incision into the chest wall: you cut all the way round the chest to open it up. This then allows you access to the sac around the heart, where you make another cut so that you can remove the clot. You can then start direct massage to the heart with your hand. It is a sort of open-heart surgery. I had never used it and wanted to tick it off my list at the earliest opportunity. It's times like that, sudden realisation when you know you're not experienced though you're familiar with the theory, when you're terrified that you won't be able to carry out the procedure for a patient in need. George was aware how I felt and promised to teach me at the earliest opportunity.

The helicopter is as stylish as it is substantial, painted in the red and white of Virgin's colours and splashed with their logo. But looks are not everything; it can reach anywhere within the M25 boundary in just ten minutes. That is unbeatably fast. It is as efficient as it gets considering the volume of 999 calls coming into Waterloo – around 2,500 a day for the area inside the M25. At Christmas time that increases: in December 1999 it was 4,500. Over the Millennium celebrations it was even higher. To deal with that volume of emergencies there are 70 ambulance stations in London and 400 vehicles on the road, plus HEMS and the BASICS doctors, volunteer medics who can be called in to help by the ambulance crews.

Ground crews are fine most of the time, but London is congested and speed is of the essence with traumatic injury. There is what's known as the 'golden hour', the first sixty minutes after the initial event. If treatment can be started within that time, then the chances of survival rise dramatically. What happens to a patient during that time affects not only their survival but also the likelihood of long-term disability. It is a one-hour window of opportunity, and it is absolutely crucial. By the time the ambulance crew arrive (assuming there is no doctor on scene), sort out the patient and get to hospital, 45 minutes have already been lost. That only leaves 15 minutes of the golden hour for treatment. HEMS has a doctor on scene within 15 minutes, after which there is three-quarters of the golden hour left to work on the patient.

Once on scene the doctor is able to do more for those who are injured than the paramedics. Paramedics can use entonox (laughing gas) and nubain, but doctors are allowed to give stronger analgesia such as morphine and ketamine. Doctors can also anaesthetise and perform procedures on patients at the roadside, doing life-saving medical work such as the thoracotomy I was to do on Stephen Niland.

It is a fact that the speed and level of expertise the HEMS team can offer not only saves lives, but also reduces the chances of long-term disability. Among the survivors of severe head injuries, 84 per cent of those treated by HEMS return to full and active life compared to 67 per cent whose treatment is by another route.

With a helicopter as its transport system, HEMS can take patients to the correct hospital for their injuries, one that could be an hour away by road ambulance. This is an aspect of the service that is really important. The helicopter can transport severe cases to either the Royal London in Whitechapel or King's in Denmark Hill. Both of these hospitals are major trauma centres that have the facilities to deal with everything. To be listed as a trauma centre you have to offer three main services: neurology treatment for damage to the nervous system; cardio-thoracic for the heart and lungs; and orthopaedic, for bone injuries. When the helicopter's operational base became the rooftop of the Royal London, the hospital itself was upgraded and re-equipped as a level-one trauma centre. There is an express lift, for sole use by HEMS, that takes patients directly from the helipad to the Resuscitation Room on the ground floor where they are treated by the A&E trauma team.

The facilities available in London hospitals comprise five neurological centres, seven cardio-thoracic departments and three burns units. There are only two multidisciplinary centres: the Royal London, north of the river, and King's, south of it. The others are all missing some vital part of the equation.

Road ambulance crews can only take the patient to the nearest hospital. It makes no difference if there is a bad head injury and the local hospital has no neurological centre. This is largely because the crews are not trained to make the diagnosis and subsequent decision that is based on it. When HEMS doctors arrive they are expected to go to wherever they think is best for the patient. Apart from the benefits of the initial golden hour, this is probably where the medical helicopter has the biggest impact.

Trauma cases are extremely expensive for hospitals. They need a great deal of expert input and require a lot of hospital bedtime, recuperation and rehabilitation. People with multiple fractures and tissue damage may need to go back to theatre time after time. It can be months, even years, before they get back to any kind of normal existence. The medical profession can be quite possessive over dealing with trauma.

Quite often there is a feeling of ownership – this should have been dealt with in my hospital – which was the nearest one to the incident. But they flew it back to the Royal London. That kind of comment I guess is natural enough – possession, ego, ownership of territory, ability subliminally questioned.

There is no doubt that trauma offers some of the most interesting, exciting and rewarding work in medicine, so it's not surprising that a local hospital A&E team can feel somewhat undermined by HEMS. But in reality no one is undermining anyone or stealing anyone else's patients, a charge that is sometimes levelled at us. If a patient has a head injury, why take them to a hospital that is not able to deal with head injuries?

With the introduction of the helicopter service a new system has evolved, one that is more advantageous to the patient, which is why we're here in the first place. In reality less than 20 per cent of trauma patients are flown back to the Royal London, and that has the hospital working almost to its capacity.

There are going to be changes to the way in which trauma is dealt with in London when the results of the Severe Injuries Working Group are published. It is looking at how these patients should be dealt with in future. This is the first time that the management of NHS trusts and government agencies are taking trauma and the effects thereof seriously. There are no definite recommendations so far, but various schemes are under consideration, such as designating certain major hospitals to deal specifically with trauma, and boosting the trauma services in the smaller hospitals so that they can deal with more cases. Hospitals such as the Royal London, King's College, St George's, Charing Cross and the Royal Free could become the five leading centres for trauma management, or it may be a north/south of the river, two-hospital model. Whatever they choose, funding for these types of patients will be more central and there will be less arguing about who pays for what when the accidents occur. As I have said, the cost is a major issue for local health authorities because trauma patients are so expensive to treat.

But it is not just hospitals bickering between themselves about how best to treat trauma, or who picks up the tab. There are problems between individual doctors as well, not on scene but once the patient is delivered to hospital. There can be criticism from other doctors when you deliver the patient to hospital. Why did you intubate this patient? Why did you do this? Why didn't you do that? People not exposed to the initial incident, with its pressures and requirement for instant and accurate decisions, can be quick to pick holes in treatment given. The only important thing, given we're all part of the NHS, is that the patients get a good deal. By the end of my six months I felt I could say, hand on heart, that I had personally come across (or heard about from my colleagues) numerous people still alive who would be dead today had it not been for HEMS.

Critics tend to throw this back at us and say: 'Yes, that's true: there are a lot of patients in a persistent vegetative state.' One HEMS doctor described how he took in a patient, a man who'd been hit by a train, and was immediately accused of over-managing the patient because he had intubated him. Right from the start I was warned that we would get criticised, even by people who knew us, and that sometimes it would be necessary to defend ourselves, to point out the realities of attending the scene – the situation on the ground, the difficulty in making clinical decisions in those kinds of circumstances; equally to point out just how easy it is to be critical in retrospect, and remind certain doctors that they weren't there, so how could they possibly know?

Professional criticism never quite goes away, though I feel it is born more of ignorance than actual petty jealousy. Sometimes, however, it exists for good reason, for example when a ground ambulance brings a patient into A&E they are delivered to the casualty doctors by a paramedic so the patient is either unconscious from the incident or awake. Anaesthetists, understandably, can get very edgy when we bring in a patient who is already intubated. They like to be there from the start. They need to know how difficult it was, the state of the vocal chords and how visible they were, so that if they have to reintubate the patient for whatever reason, they have an idea of the territory they are treading. But the fact is that without HEMS the patient might not be there at all, so we all have to accept that and find a way through our differences.

Despite all the internal wrangles that beset the service HEMS is probably one of the most successful innovations in A&E medicine in the last ten years. With all its advantages anyone would think that a service like HEMS might be provided not only in London but also nationwide. But so far it is not, and as far as I know there are no plans to extend it. Of course it is not always an essential requirement, because it is only with major trauma that it is vital for a doctor to comprise part of the on scene medical team. The rest of the time the paramedic and the ground-ambulance crew are more than capable of coping. But for a city like London using the helicopter is ideal: four doctors, in the Medic One and Medic Two teams, can cover the whole city. That seems to be enough to cope with the average of four to five trauma cases that occur each day. A battalion of doctors on stand-by would be neither necessary nor cost-effective. But HEMS does not exist in other large cities such Birmingham and Manchester, where it would probably be very useful. It would need a key player there to get it off the ground, someone who really believed in the benefits of the service and was prepared to fight for funding and sponsorship, much like Alastair Wilson did in London.

Obviously air ambulance services exist all around the UK, although HEMS is the only one to carry doctors as permanent members of the team. It is important to distinguish between an air ambulance and a helicopter emergency medical service. With the latter you are actually providing a doctor specifically trained in advanced medical techniques. An air ambulance is just like any other ambulance, except that it is able to access isolated areas very quickly. The down side is that, much of the time, you still have only a paramedic team dealing with the patient, and they are limited in what they can do. Sometimes it might just as well be a road ambulance for the difference it makes. The most seriously injured patients need to be anaesthetised and intubated, and a paramedic is not able to do that. The medium-serious injuries get done faster, which makes a lot of sense, but it can be more comfort-zone medicine, not really life saving, like HEMS.

The air-ambulance scheme with Automobile Association sponsorship is a good idea: it has pledged £14 million over the next three years to establish Britain's first national network of air ambulances, but perhaps it has been approached from the wrong end. It seems to have started with buying the machinery, the helicopter, and then worked down to the patient, rather than thinking of what the patient needs and working back from there.

In the UK thinking like this means that we lag behind Europe. In Germany, for example, every patient is guaranteed a doctor within 15 minutes, and therefore there is an air-ambulance station every 50 kilometres. The AA is still in discussion about whether or not their air ambulances will eventually carry a doctor. However, if all this is not yet resolved, at least it is being considered. I suppose there will always be teething problems with new ideas.

I was having some growing pains of my own those first few weeks in my new job, mostly as a result of the huge amount of information I had to absorb in such a short space of time. On my first day I was handed the HEMS Registrar Training Checklist. It is a list of everything I needed to know about working for HEMS and consequently it's very long indeed. During my four-week training, when I was also out on scene shadowing an experienced doctor, I was to tick everything off that list item by item, situation by situation.

There was also the strict HEMS etiquette to get my head around, the correct way of doing things. This was all written down in the manual of Special Operations Procedures, produced with team input by Gareth Davies and Tim Coates. The manual is kept in the office next to the helipad, and by the end of my training I had to know it inside out. It defined the dos and don'ts of the job, which had to be adhered to with diligence. There was the get-your-hands-dirty side to the job, as well; all the medical kit to familiarise yourself with. The other doctors took it in turns to teach me, which meant I had a pleasing row of ticks on my checklist.

If some piece of equipment or procedure broke down when I was a solo doctor on scene I had to know how to fix it. There were no rehearsals beyond my training period. The lights were up and the show was on. Anything that failed to work when I was Medic One, I had to know how to circumvent.

On top of all the knowledge I had to be fit enough to carry the medical packs from the helicopter to the scene of an accident. The big orange Thomas pack is shoulder-achingly heavy at around forty pounds, but without it I couldn't do my job. Part of the initiation into HEMS is to check these packs, and it is a thankless task. Down in the godforsaken major-incident room deep in the bowels of the hospital, seven of them are stored. In between calls during my first week I had to check them, make sure everything was present and correct. It took me hours and hours.

The Thomas packs are stored in a secure place until they are needed, at which point they are transferred directly to the helicopter. They are restocked and re-tagged after a mission in a joint effort between the doctors and the paramedics. It is as important as attending the patient on scene. There's no point in going without the right drugs and equipment. We use the supplies, so it is up to us to make sure that everything is up to scratch. Every month we would vet all of the packs to make sure nothing was missing and the drugs were up to date.

It was non-stop activity, both mental and physical, but all very sociable and accompanied by endless cups of tea. There is a lot of administration, and I have yet to meet a doctor who likes administration, especially the pack checking. But it is essential, because the pack supplies are so finely tuned that we could not risk being without something on scene: it could make the difference between life and death.

Other people's lives depended on me knowing the ropes. Even so, when I found myself on scene and under pressure, it took a while for things to become second nature. My initial four weeks on the helipad were spent getting myself into shape so I knew everything about what made HEMS tick. It was an important month, a steep learning curve, at the end of which I had to feel able to do everything myself. As soon as I was Medic One, out on the street and trying to save a life, I had to know what to do on any given occasion. It would be me and only me. Self-reliance in the most extreme of circumstances, when questions would really start to be asked. I would have to cope. There would be no one else to turn to.

9 High Flyer

THE LEVEL OF RESPONSIBILITY that lay ahead of me was alarming yet exhilarating. I was thrilled to be there, and as I waited for the bells to go off on my first day of flying, my senses tingled with excitement, the adrenaline bubbling just below the surface. They did not ring though, not that first morning, and they were still silent by the middle of the afternoon. I kept muttering to myself: 'I'm not going to go today. I'm not going to fly.'

Any London rooftop is an inspiring place: above the city looking down, ten million people spread out below you. The roof of the Royal London is no exception. You can see for miles, and you never get tired of it or take it for granted. A pair of binoculars are kept in the Ops office: Richard Camilleri, the Senior Operations Manager, still uses them to work out what is what on the skyline, even though he's been there for years. Richard used to work in the middle of the Thames, as an aircraft controller on a barge near Blackfriars Bridge that was used as a helipad. Based there for a long time, he always felt it was as good a work location as it gets till he got the job at HEMS. Then he found one even better. The view from his desk is breathtaking during the day, but it is particularly splendid at night, especially at dusk, when the helicopter sits out front with its lights glimmering just before take-off, illuminated and droning, like a metallic mechanical butterfly.

On my first shift I was shadowing George Little who, as an A&E doctor like me, was on a similar career path. It was his job that I would be taking over when my month of training was up. After my run-in with the pigeon I had arrived at 7.15 a.m. – well before the start of my shift. I must have been keen because I'm rarely on time, let alone early, for anything. I parked my moped outside the Royal London and walked into the grounds and through an entrance just to the right of the main hospital building. It is one of the largest general hospitals in England, and part of it dates from when it was founded in 1759. Behind it stands a colossal bronze statue of Queen Alexandra, and opposite is a memorial to Edward VII, erected by the Jews of East London.

Whitechapel itself is situated immediately east of the City of London, and is part of the borough of Tower Hamlets. At the end of the nineteenth century it was described as the Eldorado of the East, because of the influx of immigrants who lived and worked there, turning its streets into a vast market of stalls and street vendors. You could buy pretty much anything there. Jewish settlers landed there throughout the nineteenth century, most of whose descendants have moved on to other areas of London. In their wake they made way for a thriving Bangladeshi community. Whitechapel today is a mishmash of commercial and residential dwellings, with office developments creeping out from the City. There is an abundance of Asian owned shops, with most of the cockney Londoners having moved further east to new housing estates that spread into Essex. It is an uneasy mix of old and new and, right in the heart, when you emerge from Whitechapel underground station you can see the HEMS helicopter perched on the roof of the Royal London Hospital.

I took the lift to the fifth floor and walked up the next flight of stairs. I then passed through a series of security doors to get to the HEMS offices adjacent to the helipad on the sixth floor and rooftop of the more modern annex to the hospital. I changed into my orange flying suit and boots for the first time, relishing the feel of the cloth over my clothes. It marked me out in the world of A&E. This was the sharp end, at last, after months and months of waiting. I was here, suited and booted, just waiting now for the call.

My first duty though, was to go to the fridge to check that all the stored drugs were within the correct date. I had to draw up and prepare the anaesthetic drugs for that day, so that when a call came in we could just grab them and run.

After this it was just a matter of waiting – sitting around and waiting. And we waited and we waited and we waited. I had not felt so excited in years. The anticipation was intense, listening for the sound of that bell, the prospect of flying, of being part of the team in that helicopter. But nothing happened. In the end I began to let my frustration show, began to bore everyone, sighing from time to time.

'They're not going to call us, are they. They're not going to call us out.' I slouched there with a glum expression on my face, convinced all the anticipation, the adrenaline, would be for nothing. But the others looked at me and shook their heads and told me quietly and firmly that at some stage today we would get the call and go.

And then the alarm went off and I jumped out of my skin. I stood there for a moment then I dashed to the toilet – the last thing you want to do is arrive on scene needing to go for a pee. We would all rush to use the toilet, and once there it was a nightmare because of the flying suit. The guys could just unzip theirs, of course, but I had to all but take mine off completely. Invariably the bits and pieces of equipment would fall out of my pockets: pens, my mobile phone, stethoscope.

It was your average dismal day in England, a cold afternoon in April, and because it was cold I was wearing my tracksuit bottoms and a jumper underneath my flying suit. When I finally got myself zipped up again and ready, I collected the drugs from the fridge and one of the large Thomas packs from the storeroom. I was then supposed to walk very calmly up to the helipad. I found this hard: the excitement was so great that I wanted to take those stairs two at a time and leap aboard the helicopter.

As soon as the siren sounds, that dreadful piercing tone that makes your heart thump with adrenaline, the fire crew step smartly from their office on the platform below the helipad and take up positions around the helicopter. Some of the firemen have been there a long time because, unlike the doctors, they are on permanent contracts. As HEMS uses a raised helipad their presence is a legal requirement. Whenever the aircraft takes off or lands two of them are on stand by with hoses at the ready. When you land at ground level this is not necessary but, when you use the roof of a hospital as your launch and landing site, it is vital. The fire-fighting equipment is formidable. There is enough foam to fight any fire for at least thirty minutes. Imagine the implications of a raging inferno on top of a building full of sick people.

Along with the fire crew the captain arrives to start the helicopter engine. Richard Shuttleworth is the longest-standing pilot, all of whom are also on the permanent payroll. Richard has been with HEMS from inception, eleven years in all. As he likes to tell us, he arrived before the aircraft. All HEMS pilots are navy trained and used to landing helicopters on ships in the middle of the ocean. They find landing in London no problem, and many have done so in Oxford Circus, Trafalgar Square, Piccadilly Circus and even in the grounds of Westminster Abbey. At the Cannon Street rail crash in 1991, the aircraft landed between the railway lines at the end of the platform, before carrying three of the most seriously injured back to the Royal London.

According to Richard, the most interesting part of flying a helicopter is the take-off and landing. It is landing, however, that requires the real skill, and that's what he enjoys the most. None of it appears difficult for men of their experience.

Richard has 32 years of flying time under his belt, having qualified as a pilot with the Royal Navy in 1968 and flown extensively in the Middle East and Southeast Asia. As with every military pilot, he has experience of fixed wing aircraft and also has 70 hours in a Chipmunk to his credit.

Richard enjoys flying. He says he gets just as much satisfaction out of flying safely as he would do by performing air-display routines, and he rarely gets bored. But it is not just the flying. There is a point to it, a serious edge to it all. He told me once that every time you fly with HEMS, the chances are that you're going to improve somebody's life, or even give it back to them.

Richard once landed in a raised flowerbed of begonias and pansies in full bloom, just by the northern exit from Black-friars Bridge. His own skills particularly impressed him that day, because not one of the plants was uprooted or blown away, the wheels had even come down in the rows between the bedding stock. He has a photograph of himself tiptoeing through them. Richard also has a photo of a landing he made in Oxford Circus, which he keeps on his desk at home. He and the other pilots are sometimes accused of doing this kind of high-profile landing as a pose for the television crews or newspaper photographers. That is rubbish, however. The pilots only land in busy public thoroughfares if it is absolutely unavoidable. When Richard describes sitting up there in the helicopter above the crowds of watching people being held back by the police, descending through a hail of camera flashes, his face lights up. He freely acknowledges that he wouldn't be human if he denied the buzz he gets, the rush of emotion that comes with that level of acclaim and attention.

The last time he landed in Oxford Circus was to assist a severely injured tourist who had gone under the wheels of a taxi while looking the wrong way as she crossed the road during a shopping trip.

I was one of the doctors on board the helicopter that day. I was still in training and working alongside Alastair Mulcahy.

Richard dropped us off but, due to traffic congestion, was unable to remain there. It was only a couple of minutes to return to Whitechapel, so he took the helicopter back. Twenty minutes later we called him back to Oxford Circus to collect the patient. Once the police were informed and had dispersed the crowds, down he came. Alastair was standing in the street when the helicopter arrived, and he took a photo of the landing from the street, the same photo that sits so proudly now in Richard's study at home. It's a great shot, very dramatic: the helicopter coming down in the middle of the nation's capital. But there's an amusing side to it, a comment on life in the late-twentieth century. The helicopter is coming down between the grand buildings that edge the Circus. In the distant skyline you can see the needle-like spire of Nash's All Soul's Church and the street is solid with shoppers. But what is surprising is that while you can see one or two people with their heads tilted skywards, most of those in Oxford and Regent Streets are just getting on with what matters most to them: their shopping. It appears nothing would distract them from that, the majority are strolling along as if a helicopter landing in their midst were an everyday occurrence, a normal part of central London activity.

That landing was a moment of immense satisfaction, glory if you like, for Richard, but he is only too well aware of its serious side. HEMS place enormous emphasis on stressing that their pilots must not attempt to land in too confined a space. The saving of one life is not worth the risk of killing bystanders, or the crew, or ruining the helicopter. It is an unacceptable public-safety risk, especially when the patient may not survive anyway. Any such incident would be a massive setback for the HEMS concept in general, and it would quickly lose favour with the sympathetic and supportive public. Fortunately there have been no serious accidents and Richard finds most people are still impressed with the flying skills of the pilots, even if the landing site is the size of Hyde Park!

The landing rules have been enforced stringently in recent months. The management conducted a study to see what sort of landing sites its pilots were using, and they decided that some of them were too small. A new chief pilot brought about a reassessment of the rules during the year I was there, which was not necessarily a popular measure, albeit carried out with the best of intentions. Among others, Cambridge Circus, distinguished for little other than the terracotta façade of the Palace Theatre, once the English Opera House, was physically measured and ruled too small.

It doesn't make any real difference to the pilots where they land, because it is the medical team's problem how far away from the accident the helicopter touches down. As far as the doctors are concerned if the pilots land some distance away, we will either have to get a lift from the police or hitch a ride with a passing motorist. I have literally flagged down cars on the road. I took the bus once, and a black cab. Failing all that, you run. And fast. You can imagine with that pack on your back, a long sprint is the very last option.

The pilots acknowledge that the doctors have some fairly heavy kit to carry. They would prefer to land us right next door, but safety has to be top priority. Though we're a tight-knit team the helicopter is basically run as a public-transport system. There should not technically be any special concessions on the flying side of things just because we're HEMS. Safety has always been paramount.

HEMS employ five pilots at any one time. Obviously they rotate in a duty roster. Although they're not medically trained, they often help us carry our gear, or help out at the scene – hold a bag of fluid, for example, if we're short of hands. They know what we're going to do because they have seen it so often. No one stands on ceremony. No one ever refuses their help although the powers that be do not condone it because of the legal implications should something go wrong.

Right at the very beginning of my time there, when I was still in training, there was an accident with two patients in the one car. The doctor who was training me went off with the paramedic to attend the first patient – a man who was very seriously injured, and I took the other one, a woman. Attending her proved awkward and I needed a hand: one of the pilots, Alastair McGill, came and helped me out, watching the monitor and keeping me informed of her pulse and blood pressure at regular intervals. He was brilliant, and I would have struggled without him that afternoon.

The helicopter flies according to the rules of the Civil Aviation Authority, and is not officially meant to fly below 1500 feet in a built-up area. Because it is HEMS and has its medical remit, the rules are not so stringently applied, and it often flies lower, particularly in good weather, when the visibility is better. Our upper limit is 2,400 feet – anywhere above takes you into different airspace and different control parameters where the airliners operate. Usually there is no need for the HEMS helicopter to occupy their airspace, but it does have special dispensations when it flies on MediVac – it is then that HEMS can, and has, stopped air traffic at Heathrow.

I had assumed that the pilots flew by using their instruments, something computerised or technical like that. They don't, they just look at the roads and refer to an *A to Z* to work out where they are. It is fascinating. They do, however, use a particular street finder – *Nicholson's Street Atlas*, which is the source of all the location references. The average flight in HEMS is something like six minutes, and that includes take-off and landing. There is no speed limit in the air other than its own maximum of 200 mph, which cannot be exceeded for aerodynamic reasons. The helicopter can fly from one edge of the M25 to the other in less than 15 minutes.

I stood on the helipad and admired the helicopter as I waited to board. It looks impressive, and its track record is equally so. The figures up to August 1998 exceed 10,000 missions. Out of 1,308 missions in 1997, HEMS took or escorted 709 patients to hospital, while a further 363 were treated at the accident site. Of those carried, at least 25 would certainly have died if HEMS had not been scrambled. It is estimated that since 1989 well over 200 lives have been saved.

I felt proud to be part of it all that afternoon as I stood next to George and Sean, the paramedic, waiting while the chief pilot got the rotors turning. His co-pilot was coming down the steps from the Ops office with the Mission Briefing and HEMS Call Out sheets in his hand, job details that had just been run off the computer. We climbed on board and as soon as we were airborne the co-pilot passed the information sheets over his shoulder.

The details of the accident come over the phone from Central Ambulance Control. They are typed on to the computer by HEMS Ops at the Royal London, from where we get the final printout to study in the helicopter. The information itself is minimal: a thumbnail sketch of the patient in the box labelled Incident Details, which also logs the time London Ambulance Service first got the call, and the HEMS activation time.

It was 16.37 to LAS, 16.41 to HEMS – the length of time I had been waiting for my first call on my first flying day was now printed in exact terms. It felt like a lifetime had passed.

The location was in north London. Not only are the street and post code supplied but also the *Nicholson* page and grid references. This case, like all the rest, had its own mission number, written in a box at the head of the form next to the date, together with the name of the captain on duty. As we flew north, I read the mission briefing incident details: pedestrian hit by car, head and leg injuries. That was all – the bare essentials and no more. HEMS is a challenge to any doctor in that no two cases are ever alike, and you have to act according to the conditions you find. Once you have taken care of the basics – made sure the airway is clear, the lungs are working, and that the circulation remains stable – you have to be flexible and innovative. HEMS also operates at a different pace. Working within a condensed time schedule out on the street is not the same as treating someone within the four walls of an Accident and Emergency department. There are no familiar surroundings, staff or equipment. You have to think on your feet, be more self-reliant and informed.

This is where the HEMS call-out sheet that accompanies the mission briefing was indispensable: on it was all the data we needed on prospective hospitals. Each call-out sheet is individually tailored for the case, giving the exact location of the patient, together with the nearest treatment facility. We knew that on this occasion the nearest hospital was the Whittington in Archway Road, with the second nearest being the Royal Free in Hampstead. Then there were the nearest specialist hospitals: Paediatrics (Whittington), Cardio-thoracic (University College Hospital), Neurosurgical (Royal Free), Burns (Chelsea and Westminster) and Multi-disciplinary (Royal London).

Depending on what is wrong with the patient we know instantly which is the most appropriate hospital to take them to. If we needed the facilities of the Royal London, we would fly because of the distance involved. If we opted for the Whittington we would use the on-scene road ambulance, which would be quicker than the aircraft over the shorter distance as there would be no landing or taking off time. It is important to have the information and options in your head before you arrive on scene, so we study that *en route*.

We had taken off within two minutes of the alarm sounding and the call coming through from CAC with the information sheet. If there was anything extra we needed to know it could be radioed to us. I did not even realise we'd lifted off from the helipad, because I was too busy reading the mission briefing. When I glanced up I gasped – we were flying.

On this mission, though, and for the next two or three days, I was there only to help out. I was observer, and not expected to do anything much. George suggested I sit back and enjoy the flight, because this was the only time I would be able to do so. Once I was installed as Medic One, I would be far too preoccupied. I took him at his word, and though it was a cold and cloudy April afternoon, visibility was still quite good. I was thrilled to see Trafalgar Square and Hyde Park before we flew north past Alexandra Palace. I was entranced, excited. It was all so close, so new and so different, spread out beneath me like Toy Town.

The pilots were on course right away. They know London inside out from the air, many of them have been flying over it for years, and before I knew it we were over the scene, and it was suddenly a matter of finding somewhere to land. When you land close it is called an A-Landing, further away a B-Landing and so on. On this occasion the landing site was a playing field close to the scene of the accident. I was carrying the Propaq and the fluid Pack, which meant I had five kilos of weight in one hand, and four in the other. It is hard to run when you're not able to move your arms. I am fit, but even for me, running is not easy encumbered like that. Fortunately we did not have far to go.

Ten minutes after we were activated we arrived at the patient's side which, when I thought about it later, was impressive. I was not expecting what happened next. I have considerable medical experience, and I had qualified as a doctor more than a decade earlier. I had worked in Casualty for many years by then, and I had seen any number of traumas come into the A&E department. But the difference when you actually see it on the street is huge.

This patient was an elderly pedestrian who had been hit by a car. I believe the driver had just upped and left them, so it was a 'hit and run'. I felt awful when I first saw the patient lying there. It is nothing like attending someone in A&E. The patient was fully clothed and looked as if they had just come out for a morning shopping or to meet family or friends. Someone had then just ploughed into them, not even stopping to help or face the consequences. Because you see the patient just after they have been injured, initially they may not seem to be in too bad a shape, conscious at any rate. However, they often deteriorate quickly: in the 10 or 15 minutes after your arrival.

This patient was what we would call a typical HEMS patient: multiple trauma with injuries to the head, chest and limbs. The patient was screaming and was having difficulty breathing. The pain must have been excruciating – one leg was almost hanging off, just nubs of bone, tissue and muscle. But you have to ignore it: the shock, the severity – for the moment what's important are the basics: airway, breathing, circulation.

The first thing we have to do is stabilise the neck. Someone holds the head so it does not move (as movement has the potential to paralyse), while someone else puts a collar around the neck. Then we check the airway to make sure it is clear and administer oxygen through a facemask. Next, George listened to the chest to monitor the breathing. He found that there was no air entry in one side of the chest so he anaesthetised and intubated the patient before making a hole in each side of the chest to decompress it in a procedure known as a thoracostomy.

I had seen patients coming into A&E with thoracostomies, but this was first time I had actually seen one performed. Essentially you make a two-inch incision between the ribs under each armpit and, using a pair of forceps, dissect through the muscles. Once you feel them give, you use your finger to enlarge the hole. If air has collected there you hear the noise as it is released. Quite often you can feel broken ribs and you have to be careful not to cut yourself on them. We wear surgical rubber gloves which we put on while we are in the air approaching the scene. However, they are non-sterile, so we try to prevent infection by spraying the incisions with iodine. With your finger inside the chest wall you can feel whether or not the lungs are inflating and can also feel the heart beating.

This patient also had a fractured pelvis, so we needed to apply a pelvic splint in addition to splinting the shattered leg. All of this took time – 53 minutes in total. We aim to be on scene for about half an hour; even an ambulance that goes to a patient will be on scene for an average of 20 minutes, and they do not do all these things. It is a good system, because it means that the vital work gets done in the 'golden hour' after the initial injury, so once the patient gets to hospital the trauma team can concentrate on further management.

Once we got the patient on board, I scarcely noticed that we were flying again because I was too busy watching George. He was keeping an eye on the patient as he filled in the HEMS Work Report, one copy of which goes to the hospital where we take the patient, another to HEMS for records, and usually the doctors keep one themselves. It is extremely noisy in the helicopter, and we wear headphones so we can hear instructions from the pilots and the ground-staff, and communicate between ourselves. Once on board there are facilities for the patient, but usually the most we do is look at the monitors and, in this case, we watched that the patient's chest continued to rise and fall to indicate their breathing. All you can do in the air is keep an eye on things until you reach the hospital.

It was six o'clock when we landed, fifteen minutes to get to the hospital from the scene of the accident. The pilot shuts down the rotors when we land, which takes about two minutes. We never get off with the rotor blades still turning when we have a patient on board.

The fire crew are on stand by as we land and they help us off-load the patient. However heavy or light the injured person is it usually requires four pairs of hands. We wheel them on a stretcher trolley at top speed round the edge of the helipad and straight to the HEMS lift that links directly to the ground floor and the A&E unit. Once in the Resuscitation Room, the trauma team leader takes over.

We hung around for a while that evening to see how the patient fared. This first case of mine had been a traumatic one: their age, the extent of their injuries, the callous nature of the accident. I felt uncharacteristically drained, and my spirits dipped further when I discovered that they died soon after admission. It was no surprise, but you always hope that somehow, against the odds, a person will pull through. I knew we'd done our best for them that day, and as I travelled home it was with that thought in mind. HEMS may be exciting, and you do save lives, but sometimes you lose people too, and however hardened you may feel you can not shrug it off all of the time. But the immediacy of the work gets into your blood. There really is nothing in medicine quite like it.

10 On Scene

BEFORE I FLEW AS A SOLO DOCTOR I had a lot more training to do, and some of it was with a man affectionately known as the Human Mole. Peter Falding can crawl through anything, anywhere, anytime, and he taught us how to get to someone who was stuck somewhere seemingly inaccessible: in a mineshaft, a sewer or just a broken down London basement. With this subterranean aspect of HEMS in mind I headed for the Underground Training Centre in Acton.

The London Underground comprises around 700 miles of track and nearly 300 stations. Many of these are above ground, but the majority of those within central London are built, on average, 80 feet below ground. Any railway line has the potential for danger and the London Underground is no exception. I spent a lot of time at the training centre, because a surprising number of people end up under a tube train. Some jump, some fall, and some are pushed. In ambulance terminology they're referred to as a One Under.

The emergency stopping distance of a train travelling at 35 miles per hour is approximately 400 feet, which does not give the driver time to do much except brake hard and hope for the best. It's quite common for us to have to rescue someone who is tangled up in the wheels. Though you want to do your best for them as quickly as possible, in the circumstances, you have to do so with caution.

Because this kind of suicide attempt is a sad fact of life, London Transport runs a training day on the best ways to go about extricating a person from under a train. This is where a doctor has to be if we need to treat a patient *in situ*, or assess whether they are alive or dead, or if their limbs are still attached.

By the time we get there the train is stationary and strangely silent. You hear your every movement, your very breath, as you inch along in the dark. Imagine, crawling under a tube train 80 feet underground looking for somebody who might be dead or totally mutilated. You work your way forwards until, eventually, and with a sense of relief, you make out the silhouette of a person, a body perhaps, in the pitch black: you can see the face because the features are lighter. You've located your patient. At least you know where they are now. 'Hey, I'm a doctor. Are you OK?'

You get no answer, so you work your way closer: elbows and knees, scraping on gravel chippings. 'I'm a doctor. I'm here to help you. Can you hear me?'

Still no answer. You can see a head though, they must be unconscious. Then you get closer still and the face is turned towards you. Their eyes are open, but then you see there is no life in them at all. The body behind is heavily damaged as well, letting you know they're dead.

At the training centre there was a minimal amount of room, but I could slide along on my stomach beneath the tube train we practised on. If you were claustrophobic it would be a nightmare. You have to crawl under a section of carriage for 35 feet, along the stone chippings so that you know what it feels like and what your limitations are down there. I can do most things. I have done parachute jumping and white-water rafting, but I had to force myself to crawl the length of that train.

There are things that bother you even if you have no fear of confined spaces. For example, the helmet you wear for protection means that your head will not face front because there isn't enough room. You have to crawl with it turned to one side, not looking in the direction you are going. When I started off I was looking forwards and my visor got stuck in the gravel, and so did I, finding myself all at once unable to move either forwards or backwards. That's when the course leader talks you through it. 'If you turn your head to one side you'll free your visor. Then go back as you were and carry on.'

It's all about training and experience. If I had not had that dummy run and I got stuck in a live situation, I would not only have been very scared, I would never have reached the patient. I rate this as some of the scariest training I ever did. It felt as if the whole thing was moving, the weight shifting and everything coming down on top of me. The most chilling thought was that if something went wrong there was nothing I could do about it.

Next, in a series of role-plays, we simulated extrication. Someone volunteered to go under the train, and a paramedic, doctor and fire crew went in to assist. I climbed down to assess what was wrong, and according to their injuries how I could best move them, or if I could at all. Back on the platform I directed proceedings. I crouched beside the train with a little torch and oversaw the execution of my planned extraction. Once again I saw how limited our options were when working in such confined spaces.

Sometimes, if the patient is really tangled up, you have to get London Transport to switch the electricity back on and roll the train off them. Obviously, if they are alive and you plan to do this, you may need to leave a paramedic or doctor down there with them. It is then important to ensure that neither the patient nor any of the medical team gets hurt. The trains weigh 200 tons, and there is the serious risk of electrocution. On top of that, a fairly high percentage of One Unders have mental-health problems, and can lash out at whoever is trying to help them, which increases the risk.

What was impressed upon us most forcibly was that we should never, if we could possibly help it, stay down on the track if a train was about to move, in which case the only thing you can do, given that the train has already rolled over the patient, is sedate them as necessary and climb back up to the platform.

The first thing you do on arrival at the station is establish that the power is off. Then a circuit breaker must be put down each side of the train. In the station the positive rail is always situated furthest from the platform, but between the stations it can be on either side. However, there are still a few exceptions to this rule, and you can never afford to take any chances or anything for granted.

I learned where the switches are to turn off the electricity, who is responsible and can deal with it, and by which of the myriad phones to reach them. Rail Track does not operate the same system, so you need to know the difference. When somebody goes under a train and all hell breaks loose, you often find that another member of the public tries to leap down to help them. If the power is still on, you could be looking at two casualties.

You wear special gloves to protect your hands, because ordinary rubber ones do not save them from being cut to pieces on the ballast. The sleepers are a problem too, because they are coated in oil to preserve them so they can be horribly slippery. You end up filthy dirty, in a confined space and working with the most grisly injuries. I attended quite a few patients under trains during my six months with HEMS. Some fall, but usually they jump. Some stations have a pit so there is more depth to work in below the train. In these places the patient stands a better chance, as the train can go straight over them.

Sean Clarke and I attended a One Under where we found the patient, an elderly person, wedged in the pit under the train carriage, cackling. They were mad as a hatter and totally unscathed. We only had to coax them out verbally. Of course if there is no pit then the result is usually much bleaker. Sean used to make me laugh because whenever we were called to a One Under he would pray it was Green Park. There the gap between the base of the carriage and the track floor is so huge you can almost walk in and out. The training was excellent, and by the time we were finished I felt that disappearing into the bowels of the London Underground would be nothing like as daunting as I had felt it to be before.

Tube stations are not the only places to go crawling, and after directing the operation to extricate my patient, I took part in a Confined Space Rescue course, designed to teach you how to rescue people who are trapped in tunnels or lifts. We had to crawl through an old mine shaft. That was fine for me, being small. I could just about do it on my hands and knees, but most of the men had to lie flat and then wriggle along on their stomachs like snakes, with the ceiling pressed against their backs. I thought I would feel claustrophobic – but I found that if I kept my helmet light switched off so it was dark and I could not see anything, I was fine. I just worked my way slowly along the tunnel in the pitch black, trying not to think about where I was, aware of the monitor attached to my suit that would bleep if the oxygen levels changed.

It can be a dangerous world out there, and people have all sorts of accidents in all sorts of places. Trench workers are particularly at risk, either from the sides caving in on them, or from falling into the actual hole they are digging. It is more difficult to extricate someone than you might imagine, even from a shallow trench. Firstly, you can't stand on the side of the trench and reach down to haul them out, because the edges could cave in and the earth will fall like an avalanche on top of the person inside, burying them even deeper. That was another day's training I was glad of, having to use it later when I went to help a labourer on a building site where the trench he was digging had collapsed in on him. The other builders, everyone watching, even the ambulance crew, were standing right on the edge, peering in. I told them in no uncertain terms to move away before they buried him completely. They moved and I found the man only buried to his knees so he was not in any immediate danger, though his legs were at risk of being crushed. If he had been buried to his chest, however, he might have suffocated with the weight of the fallen earth.

The Cotswold town of Moreton-in-the-Marsh is where the fire-services training day is held. There I learned not so much about fire, as how to extricate people from upturned vehicles in road-traffic accidents. Each year in the UK 2,500 people die in what we call RTAs. A further quarter of a million are seriously injured, which equates to the population of a small town, and about 7,500 of them are still trapped inside their vehicles and have to be disentangled and rescued. All successful rescues are a marriage between medical rescue – the emergency pre-hospital treatment – and physical rescue – disentangling the casualties, often achieved by cutting people out of the wreckage. Although ambulances are mostly involved and can do both, sometimes the fire service is called in to help with the physical rescue. Statistics show how a significant number of deaths occur within the first few minutes because of major trauma. They also reveal that an equally significant number of people die between one and three hours following a traffic accident because of hypoxia (shortage of oxygen) and haemorrhage (blood loss). If a patient can be delivered to a surgeon's operating table within one hour of the time of the accident, there is a far better chance of saving their life than otherwise: it is in this critical time environment that HEMS is so effective.

Believe it or not there are cuts of automobile just like there are cuts of beef. You can slice through the A or the B post. You can cut off the sides. Or you can use a manoeuvre that slices off the top of the car much like the key does to the lid of a tin of sardines. Then there is the dashboard roll, in which you insert something that pushes away the dashboard to make space between it and the legs if they are trapped. The London Fire Brigade does not provide such intensive training, so when you arrive on scene in London, you are often the only one who knows how to do any of it. They have the equipment, but may not have been trained in how to use it or shown the best options. As a result, after my training I would often find myself directing an operation on how best to remove the doors of a car or something similar. At HEMS the one thing you learned above all else was versatility.

At the Fire Service's training day delegates took the part of casualties. Nobody told the fire crew who performed the extrication how many people were in the upturned car: they thought there was just one, but I was curled up in a ball beneath the back seat when they started smashing the windows. My face was showered with fragments of glass and I began to scream. No one heard me because of all the noise, and in any case they had made the dangerous assumption that there was only one person in the car, the one they could see trapped in the front. Eventually someone spotted me and warned the others. 'Oh, my God, we've got another patient here.'

It was only a training exercise, but I shall never forget the look of horror on his face.

That was a valuable lesson. I know what it's like to be trapped, how loud and unbearably distressing the noise and vibration is, intensified by injury. I know the extent of your fear, your shock at the accident redoubled by the fear that you might be hurt even more as you hear the cutting equipment, rattling and grinding, screeching in your ear, right by your arm your leg or your head. Sparks flying, the metal cracking and snapping like fireworks all around you. I also learned something equally valuable. Never assume anything.

I believe it's important that someone always stays with the person who is trapped, that they have no responsibility other than to be a constantly reassuring voice. 'Don't worry. We're going to do this. Do you understand? We're doing it because

. . . It'll sound awful but . . . When we're finished we're going to . . . Don't worry, I'm going to be right here with you.'

Whenever I was on scene I made sure that either a member of the fire crew or a police officer took over this task. Traffic police are good at it because they tend to be very calm, but if there is no officer available even a passer-by would do.

Depending on how badly injured the patient is, you advise the fire crew how quickly you want them out. They can literally just tear the car apart and not worry about jarring the spine if the trapped person is dying. On the other hand, if the patient is stable you can carry out the operation in a much more controlled manner, cut carefully and slide a board down the back, so that as they are pulled out you have much more control over what happens to them. It was up to me to assess how long the fire services had got, and inform them accordingly.

The other major training day I attended was at Stanstead Airport in Essex, a session on how to get people out of an aircraft after an accident: how to cut the seats back; out of which bits of the aircraft you can best extract the patient; how you use the wing. Fortunately I never needed to apply any of this, but while we were there our trainers themselves were called to an emergency incident. A plane was about to belly flop because of a failure in its wheel-lowering mechanism. Everything ended well, but it was a hairy half an hour.

I also did a shift on the road ambulances to get a feel of what the crews are able to do on scene, what equipment they have on board and how they deal with patients. I think it helps with PR too, it negates any possible hostility. I spent an afternoon at Central Ambulance Control in Waterloo, where I watched how the calls came in, how they were processed and all the procedures for call-out to the helicopter. HEMS paramedics sit in CAC so it helps to know later (when you're sometimes not getting calls) that it's not because they are not working hard enough. Some days there are very few calls or nothing appropriate at all. HEMS is a specialist service. It's part of a much bigger picture and I believe it's important to understand what other players are doing and how hard they work. The CAC staff sit for twelve hours at a time monitoring 999 calls, incredibly long shifts because they are understaffed and badly funded.

Almost every two or three months HEMS management bring in a new doctor so that someone is constantly being trained while there are between three and five fully trained doctors working on the unit. I was training people by the end of my own six months, usually Accident and Emergency doctors, or anaesthetists.

The training is vital and you learn a lot in a short space of time. Once I had completed mine I was much better able to help the doctors who were working alongside me: George Little, of course, and his colleagues Alastair Mulcahy and Laurence Gant.

My second day was sunny, and as well as a change of weather there was a change of doctor and paramedic. I was to be out with Laurence and a different paramedic, Gary Ralph. The first call was to Regent's Park, a suspected spinal injury to someone who had tripped over and fallen in the path of a vehicle.

Regent's Park is all but circular: you don't realise that fully until you approach it from the air. It is full of lakes, woodland and rose gardens, a fairy circle edged by Nash villas and terraces, but I have no idea which bit of the park we were in because you do not notice much once you get on scene. You concentrate only on the situation in hand. For example, I took one patient into a hospital when I was halfway through my six months, and the consultant in the A&E unit asked me which area of London I'd come from. I had no idea.

'But you've just been there. How can you not know where you've come from?'

'I'm sorry,' I replied. 'We just drop out of the sky. I couldn't tell you where we landed. I was only thinking about the patient.'

Flying is not like motoring, especially our kind of flying – over a city, landing in places you would normally get to by car. There are no road signs, no left or right turns, and you are only a passenger anyway, with other things on your mind. You leave the helipad, fly, and then you land. It is all over in a very short and concentrated space of time, and hence disorienting. It's odd, because though you rarely notice your surroundings at the time, another day, quite by chance, you'll be driving somewhere in the car and you realise things look familiar, and it all comes flooding back.

Anyway, we were able to land right by the patient who was complaining of a pain in his back. I could find little wrong with him. I think that because the helicopter had been called and his mates were there, he could not then say, 'Well, actually, I'm all right after all.'

We erred on the side of caution, as we always do, and took him to the closest neurological centre, at the Royal Free, just in case he had done any damage to his spine. But there turned out to be nothing wrong: no damage at all. The call had come in at 10.20 in the morning, and we were only on scene for twenty minutes, arriving at the hospital at 10.47. We decided not to fly him though, and placed him in the back of the road ambulance because the hospital was so close by in Hampstead.

HEMS does not just respond to major trauma calls, sometimes we go to a situation where there is potential for nasty injury as in the case of that patient. Sometimes there is a real problem, other times everything is fine.

During the down time between calls back at base, or on quiet days, I did paperwork – piles and piles of it. Everything has to be filed, everything has to be documented. It all has to go into the computer along with individual case notes. I used to phone around and find out what had happened to my patients. I would regularly write and thank the other emergency services, and tell them what I knew about the patient's welfare or otherwise. Additionally, we were all involved in on-going audit studies and research projects. Usually there was something to do; you never sat around twiddling your thumbs. We didn't have a cleaner on the helipad at that time, so we used to do all that as well. Then there was the equipment to check, packs to restock and retag, the drugs to monitor, checking they were all in date. All the laborious, but essential, housekeeping duties.

Day three I was an extra with Alastair Mulcahy. RTA's constitute the bulk of our calls, but we had nothing particularly gruelling that morning: an unlucky pedestrian was hit by a moped, but both he and the rider were fine. Our next call was not until the afternoon, to a labourer who had been helping to dig a trench. The digger had gone right over the man's lower leg: he was in the ditch with a compound fracture – an open break where the bones were sticking out through the wound. The driver of the digger was distraught – almost as shocked and white as his victim.

We landed in the middle of a nearby school playing field, with a huge fence round the perimeter. There was no way out near the scene, so we ended up having to run round the edge of the sports pitch to find an exit. I can climb over most things, but this wall was unassailable: brick with wire meshing and razor wire. If it had been just wire meshing, we could have clipped our way through, but as it was we had to run round the outside to get to the patient. I was carrying the Propaq monitor and the fluid pack, while Laurence had gone ahead with the Thomas pack. He kept shouting over his shoulder: 'Come on, Heather. Come on.'

I was in a terrible state, gasping for breath, weighed down, and I'm supposed to be fit. Unbeknown to me one of my friends spotted me that day, orange suited and wheezing all the way to the patient. As I worked those six months I was often seen by people who knew me, but I rarely noticed them.

Having checked that our patient had no other injuries, we concentrated on the leg. No matter what sort of injuries the patient has, you always give them oxygen. This is particularly the case with blood loss where the oxygen-carrying capacity of the body is diminished. To deal with this patient's injury it was a matter of analgesia and manipulating the leg so that we could splint it. We gave him an injection of ketamine and midazolam. Ketamine is a strong painkiller, which in higher doses can be used as an anaesthetic; midazolam is a sedative renowned for its amnesic properties – particularly useful in cases such as this. To straighten the leg I held the limb firmly just below the knee and Laurence pulled hard on the lower end. It made a horrible crunching sound that set my teeth on edge, but it is not as excruciating as it sounds because, as the bone is realigned, the pressure on the nerve endings is reduced and hence the pain with it. If left in its original position, the blood supply of the limb may be compromised and the patient could end up losing the foot or even the whole leg. The sooner you realign it, the better it is for the patient. We had got to the site at 16.26 and left the scene with the patient at 16.45, reaching St Thomas's at 16.52. That was extremely quick.

I was so enthusiastic that it didn't matter whether I was meant to be working or not, I always had my orange flying suit on and was ready to go. If ever another job came up I would ask if I could go. They usually took me, and although the fuel-to-weight ratio in the aircraft is finely balanced, I'm light enough usually not to make too much difference.

I had a few days off from flying after my man on the building site, during which time I was sent down to the major incident cupboard to check through those seven packs. However necessary, it was a soul-destroying job. These were days 4, 5, and 6, and my next flying day was not until 13 April. The aim is to give you ten flying days in your training month, and when I finally emerged from the dungeons I found myself back on the helipad with George.

What excited me that first month was that this was trauma the like of which I had never seen before. There was the flying, the jumping in and out of the helicopter, the taking off and landing. You never knew what you were going out to. It could be awful and distressing, or frustrating. It could be devastatingly sad, and sometimes even funny. Predictable it was not.

It took me a while to get used to being the focus of attention when we landed. That was unusual to begin with, but by the end of it I didn't even notice the public scrutiny. We used to go to Oxford Street sometimes if we were in the car, and I would get out to buy a sandwich. I would see people staring and wonder why. And then, of course, it would dawn on me – I was wandering around in a bright-orange flying suit.

At the beginning you are very conscious of yourself, of your suit, aware that all eyes are on you. I am not used to being seen as a performer at work; when I dance I expect people to look at the show and watch me. However, when I revert to being a doctor, I don't anticipate being centre stage or in the spotlight. But as far as doctoring goes, this job was public.

During my first month, while I was not dealing directly with the patient, just helping and observing, it was different. I had the time to look around and see what was going on. When I became solely responsible, I didn't notice anything except the patients. Every situation presented me with different challenges and I had to think on my feet: some were similar to those I'd experienced already, others were very different.

Early one morning I had said to George, 'I've never done surgery. If I have to do a thoracotomy, I won't have a clue. What on earth am I going to do? How am I going to do it?' I was petrified of being on my own with a patient who needed one. I didn't have any experience of cardiothoracic surgery, I hadn't even seen the procedure performed before. So George sat me down, and spent a considerable amount of time talking me through it. When he had finished he asked if I felt confident enough to be able to do one. I had no idea. I could understand the theory perfectly well, but was not sure that if I were actually faced with the situation whether or not I would be able to do it properly. George dismissed my doubts with a wave of his hand. 'You're a good doctor,' he said. 'Don't worry. We've all been where you are. You'll be fine.'

We were just wrapping up our session when the bells went off and we were called to an incident. When we got to the scene, we found a young man spread-eagled on the floor, blood spreading thick and dark from under him. He had multiple penetrating injuries to his chest and stomach.

Some injuries are just incompatible with sustaining further life. We knew as soon as we saw this man that his wounds were probably in that category. Like something from a movie, he had fallen on to spiked railings – we later discovered several wounds to his chest and mid-torso. When we arrived LAS were already performing life support on him, external cardiac massage, oxygen and everything else. Nothing was working. The man was dying.

But George is never one to fall at the first hurdle: he just looked at me.

'He has a penetrating wound to the chest,' he said, quietly. 'I'll show you how to do a thoracotomy, and let's see if we can do anything for him.' Where there is life, there is hope, so it was worth a try. George performed a thoracotomy, and I watched very closely. As soon as we opened him up I could see severe damage to a major blood vessel in his chest. The thoracotomy would do nothing for this man and we had no option but to pronounce him dead on scene. We left his body to be taken to the mortuary. If the victim had been a child, for example, or if there had been a distraught relative on scene, I'd have sent them to hospital. If the patient goes straight to the mortuary there is no one the relatives can talk to after they've identified the body. It's just them and their dead and that's it. That is very upsetting for anyone, no comfort whatever. If they come to a hospital there is a structure in place to help meet their need: nurses, doctors and social workers, people to talk to, sometimes to share your tears or vent your anger against.

LAS had received the call, and forwarded it on to us within two minutes. We arrived on scene within ten minutes and left again about half an hour later.

Given that it was such a horrific incident it had not affected me very much at all. Largely, I suppose, because when we arrived to all intents and purposes the man was dead, certainly unconscious. That always makes the emotional aspect of the job a lot easier. In a state of unconsciousness a patient has less of a recognisable human element. It is sad when anybody dies, and some things affect you more than others, but you can't get upset about them all. There just isn't time and you wouldn't be able to do the job otherwise. I felt relieved that I had seen an actual thoracotomy: now I knew that if I were to encounter a patient in need of one I could at least have a go. If I had not seen George perform that thoracotomy, I probably would not have been able to operate in the way I did on Stephen Niland only days later.

In the eleven-year lifetime of HEMS, some forty to fifty thoracotomies have been performed on scene. By the time I left I had done five, though some people never do one at all. It all depends on what you find when you get there. A thoracotomy is only ever performed for a penetrating wound. You never do them for blunt trauma cases, such as crush injuries or RTAs because the injuries are considered to be too widespread for it to be of benefit.

Not long before he left HEMS, George and I were called to an accident where there had been a head-on collision between two cars, and it looked so bad that after a quick initial assessment I thought neither of the drivers involved would survive. One of them did not, but after doing the basics on the other we thought she might just make it, though the chances were very slim.

As I said you never do a thoracotomy on blunt trauma. But as we were working on the driver, she lost her pulse. George inserted his finger into the hole I had already made in the side of the patient's chest, to see if he could feel a heartbeat. 'Listen,' he said. 'She's got a tamponade. The only way to deal with that is a thoracotomy.' He paused. 'There's never been a survivor from a thoracotomy on blunt trauma, anywhere in the world. What shall we do?'

It felt like he was talking to himself, though he hesitated for a moment as if he were waiting for me to answer. A tamponade is the medical term for when the sac surrounding the heart is filled with blood. You cannot survive with this condition without relieving the pressure, and the only way to do that fully is to open up the chest.

I was very new at this stage, so I felt we had to follow protocol to the letter. I advised him against it. 'But she's dead,' he said. 'And we know why she's dead – because her heart can't beat. Yes, she might have something else wrong with her, but she definitely won't survive if we don't at least try a thoracotomy. We're going to do it.'

We worked fast and furiously and released the clot around the heart.

George Little insisted on that thoracotomy and, because he did, that patient is alive and well today. She is fit and healthy, with no brain damage from the clinical death. She was the only person in the world ever to survive a thoracotomy for blunt trauma. We were the only doctors to have performed the operation with any success.

It is George's case: his decision and his responsibility. I helped him, assisted, learned a great deal. But it was George who was in charge. In different circumstances I would never have done it without him.

Technically the patient was already clinically dead. It was our last desperate hope and it worked. Nobody had ever survived this before so no one had considered it worth doing. It was a one off, one man's judgement in the most adverse of circumstances.

That case was so strange, I relive it now, the scene, the place, the smells, the emotions I went through. I had never seen George so determined, with such intensity in his face. I knew just by looking at him that somehow he was going to bring that person back, no matter what it took. The police were holding up a sheet to stop people staring as they walked by. But, on the other side of the road, a gallery of viewers watched from the balcony of a flat. In a strange, almost voyeuristic way, they were as fixated on what we were doing as we were ourselves. They had no idea of the procedure, of course, but they were absolutely riveted by our considered, if frantic, activity.

Brought back from the brink and transferred to the intensive care unit of the chosen hospital it had been a case of touch and go. Will she survive or won't she? The patient developed a very bad infection, together with all sorts of other complications, and she had other injuries as well. This case demonstrates just how on the edge the work HEMS does is. There is the opportunity to save life, but sometimes you only have a minute, or even seconds, to decide on your course of action. I was absolutely positive that woman would die, and that if she didn't she would be badly brain damaged. When a person is clinically dead, they turn a dappled mottled colour; their skin is like marble. That woman was blue, she was mottled, and she should not have stood a chance.

I do not remember much about the next couple of days, life became a constant round of patients, paperwork and yet more packs!

But I shall never forget the most mind-blowing eighteen hours I ever had on HEMS, possibly the most intense I've had in my life. It started early in the morning one Thursday, and I was working with Alastair and Gary. Our first call was at 8:50, a pedestrian, a child who had been hit by a car. She had been on her way to school with her dad and just ran across the road without looking. It was in the East End, just down the road, so we took the Audi and brought the patient back to the London.

The child was not in too bad a shape. Bizarrely, the damage to the car was quite severe. Sometimes it's like that. The car had a bullseye to the glass of the windscreen and the headlight was smashed. This kind of damage often bodes ill for the victim, but in this case she just had grazes to her left lower leg, the back of her head and face, and a swelling on the top of her head. We got her to the hospital and scanned her head, but she turned out only to have a bruise. Given that she charged into the middle of a busy London road she was lucky. She made a good recovery.

They say actors should never work with animals or children, well the same could be said of doctors. It's difficult dealing with children, and not only emotionally. It is hard to tell whether they are severely injured and therefore agitated, or simply shocked by the accident. They tend to become upset and confused and do not understand what has happened: they find it much harder to express themselves rationally than adults do. A doctor turning up in a bright orange suit is sometimes the last straw, and they can become completely hysterical. Discernment is another ability you learn when dealing with HEMS emergencies.

Our next call came in at mid-morning. A taxi had hit a pedestrian in Oxford Street. My first and only landing in Oxford Circus. I remember flying in and hovering: it was amazing. At first you think there's not going to be enough room to land, but as you get lower, Oxford Circus becomes quite a large space, big enough for a helicopter to land in. The police had cordoned off the area, so there was no through traffic. You could see right down both ends of Oxford Street as far as Marble Arch in one direction, and Tottenham Court Road in the other. The roads were lined with buses and taxis, the pavements a swarm of shoppers. As we descended past the tall buildings on the four-corners of Oxford Circus, people were staring at us from the windows. It was awesome.

I was Medic One with Alastair watching over me. 'Right,' he said. 'This patient is yours. I'm not going to help unless I think I need it. I'm just going to stand back.'

I jumped out of the helicopter with my pack on and ran down Oxford Street. The woman had been run over on its eastern stretch, down towards Marks & Spencer. You can imagine the traffic jams that built up either side of the scene and the vast numbers of onlookers. There were hundreds of people: shoppers, tourists, office workers, all of them staring.

When I got to the patient she was lying on the road with a large swelling to her head and blood oozing from her nostrils and ears. She was in a confused, and what we call combative, state: repeating herself and trying to fight us off. That can be an indication of a very severe head injury, so I decided I was going to anaesthetise and ventilate her. By controlling her breathing in this way we can ensure that her brain gets adequate oxygen – vital in any head injury. I was experienced in giving anaesthetics but here at the roadside with a million eyes on me I felt nervous. I glanced over at Alastair who gave me a reassuring nod before I gave her the injection that drifted her gently off to sleep.

Once everything was stable we packaged her up, put her on the stretcher and wheeled her quickly back to the helicopter. We took her to the London, because that was the nearest multi-disciplinary hospital.

My assumption that she had a severe head injury was correct. She turned out to have an extra-dural bleed, which is a bleed between the skull and the lining of the brain, with contusion of the brain itself. There were three fractures of her skull, two of the main part and one of the base, plus a fracture of her cheekbone. In addition she had fractured ribs with an underlying lung injury, a fractured pelvis and a fractured femur – which is the thigh bone. She was in a terrible way and all she did was look the wrong way crossing the road. But it is a common accident with shoppers in the West End, a strange city, crowded with traffic (often using the other side of the road), so we went to a lot of similar incidents.

This one at least had a happy ending. Though at first we thought the patient wouldn't survive, when I phoned for the last time a month after the event it was to find that she was doing extraordinarily well. She still had mild confusion from the brain swelling, but it was thought that that would probably resolve with time. She had her friends with her and would be returning home shortly.

The helicopter attending undoubtedly saved her life. A multiple-injured patient with the complication of a head/brain injury made speed and doctors on scene the most essential ingredients. We were able to anaesthetise and intubate her on the street, and take her to a multi-disciplinary centre, neither of which would have been possible if an ambulance had arrived on its own.

No time to rest, our next call came in after lunch. This was a severe road-traffic accident – a driver had smashed his car straight into a tree. The front of the vehicle was completely buckled and the patient was sitting in the driver's seat with the bonnet concertina-like on his lap.

We got to him by removing the roof of the car. It came off neatly, the fire brigade slicing it like the pastry lid of a small fruit tart. Once in, we managed to lift him out by using a spinal board, a big white solid plank of wood, which slides in between him and the car seat. This way his spine is protected. He came out relatively easily from the mass of tangled metal that was his car. He was taken straight to the local A&E department. *En route* apparently he complained of pain in his back, but A&E were able to send him home the same day. He was lucky – very lucky.

Sometimes something that looks so terrible – and this did look horrendous – turns out fine. We had not even needed to escort him to hospital, just put him in the road ambulance and sent him off, phoning up later to make sure he was all right.

The day was cold even for April, and I had felt chilly even before we arrived on scene. Despite all the activity I didn't really warm up, and when we got back to the helicopter, which had landed a couple of hundred yards away, I was still cold. It was a wonderful surprise to find somebody living locally had brought us all big mugs of tea. We drank them gratefully before flying back to Whitechapel again.

The fourth call came in at 4.12 in the afternoon. This was to attend an eight-year-old child who had been knocked down by a lorry. The second child of the day, but this one was awful. We landed on a patch of grass alongside the road where the lorry had come to a halt, and found the patient lying on the tarmac in front of some flats. I jumped out of the helicopter before the blades had stopped turning and raced over to the scene. To my horror I saw the little lad was still trapped by one of the wheels of the lorry, a huge articulated vehicle with massive wheels and tyres. One leg was under it, the other sticking out one side; neither was fine, but the one trapped beneath the wheel was much worse. We checked for other injuries, but there were none, and the boy could still talk. He was brave, very brave indeed, and proved to be an absolute star.

Even in that state I could tell he was mischievous, a lively little chap, sheepish rather than terrified. The child's mother was beside him. Normally in such circumstances we ask the police to take any parents or relatives away from the scene, and get someone – usually a policewoman – to stand and chat to them to calm them down. Parents are often, understandably, distraught and can do more harm than good. Once we've treated the child and got them ready for hospital, I always have a chat with them, let them know what the injuries appear to be and what we're going to do about them. It isn't usually possible to say much more at that point in time. When we are ready for the ambulance transfer, if they are calm it's better for one of them to travel with us, as a familiar face is reassuring for the child.

I had reached the end of my two days of observation, but I still had Alastair on board to keep watch over me. Though I was now officially Medic One, he was there to ensure I was OK and help out as necessary. At this point I still needed quite a lot of help, because I was dealing with things I had never seen before. With the latter case I learned that I should not get underneath the lorry until I was 100 per cent sure that it was safe to do so. The wheels had to be chocked and the engine switched off so that it could not roll and hit me or my paramedic or anyone else. It is very easy to forget in the heat of the moment and just go diving in to help the patient without giving a thought to your own safety.

I looked around at the scene of the accident. Behind me, in a line that stretched eight-foot along the road, there was grisly testament to what had happened. I could see skid marks, that showed the point from where the boy had been dragged along the tarmac. It was incredible that he was alive, never mind conscious.

Once it was safe I went under the truck and had a look. I crouched down beside him, speaking in a reassuring voice, while I thought about what was best to do. In the end, after discussion with Alastair, I decided that the only way to get him out would be to reverse the lorry off him.

Clearly this could not involve the driver, because he was sitting in a police car in a state of shock, so we asked one of the police to climb into the cab and reverse it back. That was a grim moment: the child on the ground, the diesel engine being started with a teeth-jarring rumble, then the clunk of reverse gear and it was slowly backed off the wounded boy. But there was no other way, and now we had full access to the child and the injured leg. It was obvious, as I had suspected initially, that the only way to deal with the child effectively would be to give him a full anaesthetic, so that's what I did. Before we left for the hospital I covered up both legs with iodine-soaked dressings and, as there were fractured dislocations of both ankles, I pulled them straight and splinted them. His mum came with us in the back of the road ambulance. We went to the local hospital, which had facilities for plastic surgery, orthopaedics and paediatrics, the three specialities I needed for this child.

I thought he would lose his right leg – I was convinced that there was no way that leg would survive. However, it never ceases to amaze me just how resilient the human body can be, and just how good modern medicine is. Thomas made excellent progress, and when I last visited him, both legs had healed nicely. The surgeons had only to needed to amputate a couple of toes. But that was it. He would walk and play and even trampoline like any other little child again. I had been right about his nature: because even when he was in a wheelchair, he had apparently caused havoc on the wards. This was a wonderful outcome. It had been one of the worst cases I had ever seen.

What we witness immediately is often not all it seems, especially with head injuries; people who initially just seem a bit confused can turn out to have a major haemorrhage in their brain and die. It can be difficult, because you expect them to survive and when they don't the shock really hits you. There are other patients whose chances you rate as zero, who survive against all the odds. Then it is a fantastic feeling to know that you have helped them to live.

Alastair and I had survived an extraordinary day ourselves, and we were winding down in our office by the helipad. Alastair was talking me through the cases we had seen that day, discussing what else I might have done and how I could improve. We had arrived at the hospital with the last patient at 17.36, so we hadn't got back to the Royal London till quarter to seven. The helicopter went home almost immediately afterwards, Denham bound while it was still light. It was a Friday, so with no Audi on duty either, HEMS was effectively closed for the night. Debrief over we were just beginning to chill out over a cup of coffee, when the telephone rang.

11 Heli's Angel

'I F THAT'S A CALL, IT'LL BE A BIG one,' Alastair said. No one would normally phone us at that time; it was half past seven, and we were meant to be off line. Everybody else had left for the night, and we were not even supposed to be there. It had been a long day, and we were both keen to get home. Alastair had told his wife he would be back for supper by eight thirty, and I was looking forward to a quiet night in. For once I had an evening without any social engagements or dance rehearsals to attend, and I was keen to take advantage of this and relax.

I could see Alastair prevaricating slightly, hesitant as he reached out a hand for the receiver. We had just been through a tough 12-hour shift, one of the toughest so far for me, and I had been running on adrenaline most of the day. It would have been sensible to have left it, just let it ring, but I had the feel of something now, and I could not stop myself from urging him to answer it. He did and I could tell from the look on his face that he'd been right. It was Central Ambulance Control in Waterloo. He cupped his hand over the mouthpiece: 'A stabbing in Stratford Broadway. They want to know if we can respond.' He frowned slightly as he waited for my reaction, 'Do you want to go?'

'Of course I want to. How can we possibly not?'

There wasn't a shadow of doubt in my mind, even though it was so late and we were technically off duty. I was still raring to do anything that came my way. Alastair was a fraction more reluctant, cautioning me that it would mean a really late night, and I should remember that I was on duty again first thing in the morning. He had more experience than me and knew better when to call it a day. But my enthusiasm was insatiable and overcame my better judgement.

'OK,' he answered,' more determined himself now. 'But what are we going to do? We haven't got a paramedic.'

Gary Ralph, the paramedic who had been on duty with us that day, had gone home like everyone else. There was no one to drive the Audi A6 Quattro, the HEMS rapid-response vehicle that was parked in the hospital grounds. Fortunately Alastair is a BASICS doctor: these doctors go out voluntarily to accidents in their own cars. He had been trained to drive with lights and sirens and was therefore authorised to drive the Audi.

Both back in our normal clothes now, we had to pull on suits and boots once more and quickly reassemble the drugs, resuscitation equipment and instruments. We grabbed everything, hurtled down two flights of stairs to the lift and the ground floor. We threw our gear in the back of the car and jumped in. Alastair fired the engine and seconds later we were out in the rush-hour traffic, heading down Whitechapel Road, sirens blaring, emergency lights flashing, and a seven-mile drive to Stratford ahead of us.

I was navigating, and it was very busy. What a difference this was, pushing and shoving our way through the traffic with sirens and lights going full blast, when normally we'd be hovering above it all in the helicopter.

Compared to the paramedics Alastair was a very slow driver, which was a relief to me. He used lights and sirens to get through the traffic, but he did not go careering along at break-neck speed, throwing me back and forth in my seat as he jammed on the brakes and stamped on the accelerator in turn. Once, while answering a call on the A13 on a particularly wet day with paramedic Dave at the wheel, we had aquaplaned, almost losing control. I was always petrified when driving at speed in the Audi. Give me a helicopter landing in Oxford Circus any day.

We got the call at 19.50 and, despite Alastair's slightly more sedate pace, we arrived on scene at 20.06, only sixteen minutes to get from the top floor of the Royal London Hospital to the Swan Pub in Stratford. Twenty-one minutes had passed since someone dialled 999.

It had been difficult to find the pub at first because Stratford town centre is built in a big circle, so you have to go 'round the one-way system, and it was over the far side. We stopped to ask someone directions. They had no idea, but they told us there was a swarm of police cars on the other section of the one way system. We raced on till we spotted the mêlée of blue lights. The police had cordoned off the pub itself – a double-fronted, red-brick Victorian building – and the immediate area around it. We hauled the medical equipment out of the car and dashed into the pub.

The atmosphere felt strange, a sort of noisy hush: the air was thick with smoke, and it smelled of stale beer and nicotine. Friday night, the place must have been heaving before police had cleared it. Most of the customers had been moved outside; some had been shunted to one side of the pub. There were empty tables laden with half-full glasses and cigarettes still burning in ashtrays. We found our patient lying on his back on the varnished wood floor. Young, well built, at least six feet, his face strangely lit by the rainbow colours from a fruit machine. He had a drip inserted in his arm and an ambulance paramedic crouched beside him, together with Ken Hines, a BASICS doctor, who had been called directly by the ambulance service.

Alastair and I dropped to our knees beside the doctor and the paramedic. I touched the patient's skin – he was cold and clammy. There was little evidence of injury – just a small wound on the front of his chest, less than half an inch long, that had been covered with a small strip of elastoplast.

It was obvious that the man was very sick indeed. His pulse was weak and thready, his blood pressure dropping. His pupils were fixed and dilated and he was struggling to breathe – it was slow and harsh and laboured. Alastair said: 'Right, I'll intubate him, and you get on with the rest.'

I applied the blood pressure cuff and connected him up to the monitor. Alastair gave him a partial anaesthetic via the drip the paramedic had already established – just enough to paralyse him and relax the muscles so that we could pass a tube into the windpipe, secure the airway and start to ventilate him with oxygen. I focused on restoring the blood pressure. We had to establish whether or not the knife had punctured a lung, causing a tension pneumothorax, where the lung collapses to the extent that it squashes the heart, preventing it from working.

I started on the bilateral thoracostomies to decompress the chest. I took the scalpel I always carry in a pouch in my knee pocket, and made the initial incisions just under the left and right armpit. Using a pair of forceps I forced open the muscles between the ribs, completing the opening with my index finger. I could feel the lungs moving up and down. This was good news. The lungs were inflated. On top of that, it was likely that none of the large blood vessels had been severed during the stabbing, because no blood gushed from the holes that I had made in the chest.

I rechecked the pulse, my fingers seeking the beat in his neck. I found nothing. There is often a moment where you're not sure whether there is a pulse or not: whether you are just not able to feel it because it is so weak or because it's gone entirely. It is a tense few seconds. Your thoughts seesaw: Yes, I've got it. No, I haven't. What makes it harder is that you can feel the pulse in your own finger and you have to differentiate. I probed with my fingers, counted to ten, and when I still couldn't feel it, I looked at Alastair. 'No pulse.' Our patient was clinically dead.

The knife must have penetrated the heart itself, flooding blood into the sac (pericardium) containing it, and creating such pressure it could no longer pump. External cardiac massage would do no good now – our only option was a thoracotomy.

When I suggested it Alastair did not falter: 'Well, you've seen one before, you start while I go out to the car and get the kit.'

This was it. It was up to me now, and I had to act fast. The patient only had this one last and slim chance. I would open up his chest, remove the blood clots and hope to massage the heart back to life. We had just three minutes before his brain, starved of oxygen, would cease to function. With a stiff breath I took up my scalpel once more. I had already made the two holes to decompress his chest, now I had to join them up and get at his heart. I made a surface incision with the scalpel all the way across the chest, tracing from one armpit horizontally below the nipple to the breastbone and then following the same route across to the other side. This got through the skin, but to go deeper I had to use scissors. I took hold of my 'Tough Cuts' – scissors I kept in my suit, and normally used to cut off a patient's clothes.

Carefully I slid them into one of the thoracotomy holes and with my left index finger under the bottom blade to make sure I didn't go too deep, I leaned over the body and began to cut between the ribs.

I was cutting through muscle until I got to the breastbone, but muscle is sinewy and tough and thick, and it was taking valuable time. I struggled on, eventually reaching the breastbone. The scissors were not designed for this and they strained at the axis, threatening to give way and buckle or break altogether. My hand ached and I was sweating with the effort.

Alastair returned. 'Look,' I said. 'I'm going too slowly. I can't get through the breastbone. You start on the other side and meet me in the middle.

He started on the other side. He cut and I cut, struggling on with the scissors, me from the right him from the left. I wiped my brow with my sleeve and applied new pressure to the patient's breastbone. Then all at once I felt the last of the bone give. I was through.

Alastair had brought the retractors from the car: huge vice-like metal clamps that you put in to wrench everything open. By inserting them into the incision the entire chest wall is prised open in two halves. It looks like an open clamshell. Now we had a 20-inch aperture and we could see inside the chest cavity itself: not only the lungs, but the heart too. The pericardium was bulging, full of trapped blood. That was the source of the problem, common with stab wounds and deadly. The heart wasn't beating: we had to get it going again and restore the supply of oxygen to the brain. I had to release the pressure and I had to do it quickly or risk leaving him with permanent brain damage. Already we had used up two of our three vital minutes, so we had no more time to lose.

I lifted the skin on the sac around the heart with a pair of forceps. This was particularly difficult because it had stuck to the wall of the chest in places and everywhere was slippery with blood. Finally, I cut through the last of the sac and there was the blood clot. I scooped it out with my fingers, spilling it over the floor. Normally you would flick the heart or start squeezing it to get it beating again: so I put my hand in ready to start massaging and paused. There I was, Friday night, the floor of an East End pub with somebody's heart in my hands. I could feel the faintest flicker through my fingers. I hesitated, waiting. The flicker became a flutter and I waited. It grew stronger and a little stronger still. For one long moment I held my breath, seeing if it would falter, praying that it wouldn't. Then I let my breath go in a sharp sigh. 'Alastair. His heart's beating again.'

The moment of death had passed, but we were far from home yet. With the heart beating again, a small fountain of blood had begun to spurt from the hole made by the knife.

We needed to close it in some way. In hospital we would have stitched it, no problem, but here?

I began to feel uneasy because I could not see what I was doing or establish exactly where I had to repair. The blood was pumping steadily now, and if I didn't do something about it the patient would be in danger for different reasons.

'I can't see enough to sew this,' I said. I was operating on the floor of a pub. I had only the most basic equipment and now the minimal lighting was making things even worse.

Turning back was not an option. I had come too far and for the next thirty seconds or so I looked for a way to stem that blood flow and stitch up the hole. But I knew it wasn't going to happen. I realised I might do more harm than good, so brain in overdrive, I turned to Alastair, 'Stick your finger in the hole. It's our only option.'

Alastair didn't hesitate. He pushed his right index finger very gently into the heart, almost as far as his knuckle. I watched. I waited. The response was encouraging. The heartbeat was growing stronger and stronger, and Alastair could feel the twitching of one of the valves against his fingertips. Gradually the bleeding stopped, and as it did so the beat became more regular. There was nothing more we could do here. It was time to get this patient to a surgeon.

We got him packaged for the ambulance very quickly, grateful that we could do so without any neck or spinal injury to consider. We lifted him on to the trolley as fast as we could, our only real concern was keeping Alastair where he was and hence the patient's heart stable, his index finger still stemming the flow of blood.

We were wheeling him out to the ambulance when someone tripped on the drip lines we had put in. For one awful moment I thought they would be yanked out, that was the last thing we needed. Once in the ambulance, off the grimy floor and in better lighting we decided we would have another look at the entry wound to see if we could stitch the heart, but when Alastair moved his finger, a great spurt of blood shot out, soaking us and the stretcher trolley. We looked at one another and grimaced. Alastair put his finger back and that's where it stayed until we got the patient in to the operating theatre in hospital.

We had to drive quite slowly. Alastair's finger securely in place, we pushed fluid in via the drips on each side. As we did so, the heartbeat got stronger and stronger until his blood pressure returned. His pupils returned to normal size, and his colour had begun to return.

We arrived at the Royal London at 20.37 and went straight to A&E. I could scarcely believe that it was only half an hour since we had first pushed our way through the swing doors of that pub. I had radioed the hospital to warn them of our arrival. They needed to know we were coming, and I had to make sure they had one of the theatres free and a cardio-thoracic surgeon at the ready. We spent an hour in Casualty stabilising him before they took him up to the operating theatre. Alastair had his finger in the hole in the heart for the entire time. By the time he was clear he'd been doing it an hour and a half and it was completely numb.

When we got him up to theatre, the cardio-thoracic surgeon took over, initially using one of his own fingers to plug the hole. They inserted a catheter, a long tube with a tiny balloon on the end that was normally used for the bladder. Once that was *in situ* the balloon was inflated on the inside so it covered the hole. The surgeon could then stitch over the mushroom the balloon had created, after which it was deflated and removed.

When he finally came out of theatre the man was taken to the intensive care unit for the night. They had not even needed to put him on bypass. Alastair told me that he thought he was going to survive, but when I looked back to what had confronted us on the floor of that pub, the still heart, the fight against time, scissors on breastbone, I could hardly believe it.

But I tempered my emotions. It was still very early days and I had fought so hard to save this man that if he died now, with me thinking he'd live, I would have been devastated. I kept doubt uppermost in my mind. How could he possibly live? The chances were too slight and there was also the risk of infection and brain damage.

But our night wasn't over yet – we had to go back and find the equipment we had left scattered over the pub. HEMS is so poorly funded that we have very limited resources and we can't afford to lose anything. We were lucky that night because the police had collected it for us. They collated it all and brought it, and the Audi, back to the hospital.

It was about 10.45 p.m. and Alastair decided we deserved a drink. So we went to the local pub, 'the Sam' (Good Samaritan) bizarrely apt name for a pub that night. We just about made last orders. I ordered a white wine and Alastair a pint of beer, and we settled in a quiet corner. For a while we just sat there not saying anything. We were stunned. After a few minutes I glanced around at our fellow drinkers and said: 'If the people here only knew what we've just done!'

It was odd to be there, a bunch of people at the end of a night's drinking, blissfully unaware of the drama that had unfolded in a similar establishment a few miles up the road. For a while that night the Swan in Stratford had been the scene of life and death, although no doubt normal service would have resumed by the following day. Soon everyone would be drinking and chatting, watching sport on TV and playing the jukebox or fruit machine, just like they now were in the Sam. I sat back, exhausted. We had reached the end of an incredible day, a roller coaster of emotion, up and down and round and over, no respite as we dashed from call to call. Fifteen hours since it began this morning. I was so dizzy I doubted I could get off. But staring round that pub I saw the world as it really was, oblivious to where I'd just been. I came down to earth with a bump.

I had gone to work by moped that morning, but as it was now after midnight and I was in no fit state to drive, the hospital provided me with a taxi back to Queen's Park. I was at work the next day by 7 a.m. and thought little of it. Of course everyone heard what Alastair and I had done, and they were soon teasing me, supportive of course, though perhaps a little envious. There was a bit of banter and a touch of the 'It's not fair. You're the new doctor, and you've done a thoracotomy.' Everyone hopes to perform a thoracotomy during their six months with HEMS. As I said, I did five, but they are quite rare. Alastair had never done one, neither had Laurence. George had done only one prior to the blunt trauma, but the patient had not survived. Now I had done what a few days earlier would have been, to me, unthinkable. I had performed a thoracotomy, and Stephen Niland was alive as a result. Steve, as I call him now we know each other better, has the distinction of being only the fourth person in the world to undergo the procedure outside the clinical environment of a hospital and live, and only the third to survive without brain damage.

They teased me at work, but I knew they were proud. It was good for HEMS, an achievement and a vindication of the service. Apart from talking to my colleagues and an excited phone call to my mother, I said little about it.

The next day I had a call from Claire, my sister. 'Heather, you have to speak to mum. I think she's lost the plot. She's been going round telling everybody that you've been doing heart surgery in a pub. Please just phone her will you and put her right.'

I smiled to myself. 'I can't, Claire.'

'Why not?'

'Because it's true.'

That was what was funny. No one really believed it, open-heart surgery on the floor of an East End pub.

Steve came out of hospital on day six, and it was not until then that I actually allowed myself to believe that he was going to be OK. I just kept thinking about all the possible complications. Recovery from this kind of wound, this kind of operation, this kind of environment. Everyone else was enthusiastic, however, and kept assuring me he was, and would be, fine. But I didn't want to believe he was out of the woods until I had definite proof. On the morning he was due to leave hospital, Alastair and I went to see him. We arrived on the ward and asked a nurse where he was. She pointed to a man sauntering along the corridor. 'That's him, there.'

Alastair's mouth dropped open. I gulped. Yes, that was indeed him, walking along the corridor like he'd walk along the street on his way to work or wherever. He could not have looked more different from the person we had first seen less than a week earlier, prostrate and dead, lying on the floor of a pub. We followed him as he turned into the ward and joined him at his bedside. His father was standing there waiting.

That was an emotional moment. I had an overwhelming urge to cry. I didn't, but it was only just. Both Steve and his father had tears in their eyes. I stood quietly and still found it hard to accept that this picture of health and humanity was the same man we had attended with sirens and lights only six days earlier. It could have been hours previously that Alastair's finger had been wedged in the hole in his heart, to stop him bleeding to death. I don't think I was actually convinced we were dealing with the same person until Steve pulled up his T-shirt and showed us the huge jagged scar that crossed his chest from armpit to armpit: one grim and telltale line that dipped slightly underneath each nipple. He had needed 70 stitches, and the cardio-thoracic surgeon had complained that my cut was ragged!

Meeting Steve and his father was the high point of my six months on HEMS. It was then, that wonderful moment, that I allowed myself to accept, to believe that he was not only alive, but going to be all right. Steve himself had no idea that at one stage that Friday night he had been dead. I don't believe it was until we met in that ward that he appreciated fully what had happened to him.

Once we started talking he wanted to know everything, but you have to tread carefully, because it is a shock to hear that kind of thing said about yourself. It was hard not to tell him everything, though, because it was so easy to forget just by looking at him that he was only days out of major surgery.

To begin with Stephen had no idea what to say to us. Apart from thank you. What else can you say? And what could I say to him? People always asked me what we said to one another. The truth is we said very little, although we looked at each other for a long time, and perhaps looks speak more eloquently. We spent about three-quarters of an hour at his bedside before he went home. I had my camera with me, and we took some photos in the hospital, just for us.

It was about a week later that Richard heard what we'd done and suggested it might be good publicity for HEMS if we were to contact a newspaper with the story, given that it had such a happy ending. I wasn't sure it was a good idea, not certain that anyone would want to read about it, but he insisted it would get good coverage and told me he was going to phone our press department and see what they had to say.

By this time we knew Stephen was going to make a good recovery, not just survive, so I was not too fussed. Richard made his call to the communications department of the Royal London, who in turn phoned the *Evening Standard*. The following day I received a call from the newspaper asking me if I would be willing to have my photograph taken with Stephen at home on the day after he left hospital. I told them that would be fine, so a reporter and a photographer from the paper came and picked me up from the hospital after work and drove me over to Stephen's parents' house in the East End. I gave them an interview, and they took a couple of pictures of me with Steve. They said it would be out soon afterwards, possibly as early as the following day.

I thought nothing more of it, went home that night and into work the next day as usual. I was out getting lunch, standing in a queue for some sandwiches when I saw a photo of my face on the front page of the newspaper tucked under the arm of the person in front of me. 'Open Heart Surgery on

Pub Floor – Woman doctor saves life of stabbing victim' was how the headline went. I could hardly believe my eyes. I paid for my sandwiches and, half embarrassed, half proud, I made a hasty retreat back to the helipad.

The day after I was at work on the roof of the London, Medic One again. We had just come back from a job, nothing too serious, a road-traffic accident I think. As we landed I noticed a few more people on the helipad than usual and dismissed them as a PR visit. HEMS was always in need of charitable contributions, and with this in mind they sometimes showed people around. As we sat in the helicopter waiting for the rotor blades to stop spinning I was preoccupied with the report sheet on my last patient. There were still a few gaps that I needed to fill, and aspects of the case I wanted to discuss with the other doctors before I did so. When the paramedic opened the doors of the helicopter I jumped out, and was immediately faced with a barrage of clicking cameras. The helipad was crawling with cameramen and journalists, every newspaper and TV station in the country seemed to be there.

I was completely overwhelmed, and my initial reaction was, Oh, no! Don't. Go away. Even after I had got over the initial shock, I was still unsure. HEMS were very pleased to nurture the publicity though, so I willingly co-operated. The rest of the day was an endless round of interviews, photographs and filming. It was most bizarre. I had turned up to work a normal shift as Medic One and found myself an overnight celebrity. This was the fifteen minutes of fame that Andy Warhol so famously described. Only my fifteen minutes have gone on somewhat longer.

The Stephen Niland story made just about every newspaper. Alastair and I referred to the pictures as our wedding photos because we stood together in all of them. When the pictures went to press, however, Alastair didn't appear in many of them. The media must have thought a girl on her own made a better story. This sometimes made it look as if I had done the whole thing single-handedly, although reference was usually made to Alastair and the teamwork in the text. Alastair had his finger in Stephen Niland's heart for an hour an a half. Without his help Stephen may well have died. The press have left him out of some of the pieces they wrote, but this has never overly bothered him. Alastair's reward was evident in something he said at the time: 'We are absolutely delighted that Stephen has made such an amazing recovery. It is a fantastic feeling to be involved in something like that.'

At the end of that long and eventful day, after the press had finally gone to prepare their stories, I was joking with Alastair in our office. We were having the last of what had been endless cups of tea, and I suddenly smiled. It occurred to me that we were not really famous until we had made it on to the pages of *Hello!* I shared this with Alastair, and we had a good laugh about it.

I was somewhat taken aback when, three days later, who should call but *Hello!* I was out at the time, but they left a message: would I be willing to allow them to put together a four-page article on me? At first I thought it was a joke, that Alastair had put someone up to it. But when I phoned and spoke to Sarah Cartledge, I knew it was for real – no one was pulling my leg.

It was not just *Hello!* and the tabloids that showed interest, even the broadsheets gave me coverage. The *Guardian* news piece was a two-column story headed 'Knife in heart victim saved by surgery on pub floor', accompanied by a photo of me with Stephen. It also reported a Metropolitan police spokeswoman as saying four men had been arrested in connection with the stabbing and released on bail, though no one has ever been charged. In the *Daily Telegraph*, as in *Metro*, there were illustrative diagrams accompanying the story that showed how the operation was done. The tabloids were most vociferous in their acclaim, but there was an amusing slant on it all in the *Mail*, in which the writer said they were 'spellbound with admiration' for me.

Apparently they had picked up on what I'd said about how fortunate I had been to watch George Little perform a thoracotomy two days earlier and how this had given me the confidence to have a go. The fact that I had only to observe something once in order to be able to do it myself was impressive, they felt, writing as someone who themselves could not even rewire a plug, despite having watched other people do so on countless occasions.

I was inundated with requests for interviews. I was selective though, and chose things that I thought were important. I did a big piece for a blood-donating magazine with a picture and a lengthy interview, because without blood from donors a lot of our patients would not survive. We do not give it on scene unless we absolutely have to, but when they get to the hospital, huge quantities are used for trauma patients. It is the public who give it. I wanted to draw attention to this and show that – day in day out – there are patients like Steve who need blood.

I also wanted to to promote HEMS as much as I possibly could. The work is invaluable and HEMS needs as much publicity as it can get. It is nice to be in the papers on the strength of having done something positive with them. They need money all the time, resources are finite: HEMS is a charity. The TV work was great publicity, and I eventually got over being camera shy. I had appeared in public as a dancer but never as a doctor before. It was the crossover that was difficult.

We did a *999* reconstruction of the Stephen Niland case for BBC1. It was good exposure for HEMS and useful for the public to see the sorts of things we do and how we do them. *999* covers anything, fires, near misses, people who cheat death, incidents where there has been a really dramatic rescue. They reconstruct cases from HEMS when there is anything exciting to report. The filming of Stephen's stabbing took place a fortnight afterwards, and the BBC's props department presented me with fake blood and a condom filled with red currant jelly that was supposed to be the heart. I had to cut it open. It was surprisingly realistic. Steve came to watch, accompanied by both of his parents. He was fine. He remembers nothing about that night and said it was just like watching someone else on television. But his parents found it quite distressing.

Steve's parents have raised a lot of money for HEMS since the incident, and had a big charity night a month after his recovery in their local pub, the Army & Navy in Plaistow. They auctioned off Alan Shearer's football shirt and some snooker cues and cricket bats, all of which had been signed by an array of sports celebrities. They raised about £6,000 for us that night. That party was among the best I have ever been to, and I had an emotional time meeting the whole Niland family – grandparents, brothers, sisters and cousins. There are a lot of them, and they were so kind and appreciative. What was lovely was that nothing we had done was taken for granted. I have since been back to see them and Alastair and I are now honorary Nilands. The family put on another charity night in the same pub the following November, in aid of an autistic child: Alastair and I went along as guests to help them achieve their target.

That November I was honoured to be voted one of twelve People of the Year, an award that has been presented since 1959 by the Royal Association for Disability and Rehabilitation (RADAR). The winners went to meet Tony Blair at 10 Downing Street prior to the awards lunch held at the Hilton in Park Lane. There I met everyone from Jeffrey Archer to Sue Cook and had my photo taken alongside Evelyn Glennie, Jenny Pitman, Heather Mills and Barbara Windsor. I also met a team of builders, the African Project Builders, who went out to Kenya and built the Dabaso Primary School in Watamu. They had another trip planned, and wanted me to join them as team doctor. I could not make it that time, but I am still getting lots of different offers, some of which I'm able to fit into my already busy life. In February 2000, for instance, I went to the Sahara for ten days as team doctor for a MENCAP expedition. But that's a whole other book.

I was still very junior to HEMS when all this publicity broke. It was 16 April, and I'd been part of the team for ten days when I performed the thoracotomy on Stephen Niland. I had not even completed or passed my training month. From just being another doctor in an orange suit, I was suddenly on TV and all over the papers. It bothered me and I started to wonder if I was going to arrive on scene with people expecting miracles. People were going to recognise me – and of course for a while they did. They would point at me, and I would hear them mutter about TV and heart surgery and stabbings.

I really began to wonder about people's expectations. I was sure I was not going to be able to live up to them. In fact that never happened. I did have subsequent patients who died, but I never had any unpleasantness. If anything, people would come up, keen just to shake my hand and say, 'Well done'.

After that I went through a phase when I believed I could save anybody and everybody, and I refused to give up. A particular case that remains in my mind is a pedestrian who was hit by a car.

He had massive head and chest injuries. We were working on him, and I was like someone possessed, on some kind of personal mission to save him.

Eventually one of the paramedics tapped me on the shoulder: 'Stand back, Heather, and take a look. The guy is dead. You can't do anything for him.'

I looked down at what was left of the man and knew that the paramedic was right. When you have as good as brought someone back from the dead, for a while you think you can do the same for everyone. Finally I pronounced him Life Extinct on scene, but only after the ambulance crew persuaded me I must. Still I looked on. The call was over. The man was gone, but it was impossibly hard to quit, to accept defeat and just walk away.

It was a strange time: immensely difficult trying to behave normally at work again. I might have been on TV and in the pages of *Hello!* but I still had to check my packs. I got teased much more now – apart from myself and two women in data-collection, it was all men on the helipad. I had to tough it out and they pulled my leg mercilessly. It was all done in the spirit of fun, though, and I took it on the chin. They collected pictures from the papers and rewrote the headlines and attached my face to a scantily clad body found on one of the less salubrious Internet sites, pinning the pictures up on the walls of the office.

Not long afterwards, I was earning some extra money doing some time as a locum in the A&E department of an east London hospital. A man had come limping into Casualty, not able to walk on his right foot – he'd stepped on a big splinter while padding around at home. It was very deep into the sole and somehow I had to extract it. This was harder than it may seem, because the wood had gone soggy by this time, and only the tip was in view. Because it was in vertically there was nothing much to get hold of. I kept trying to pick at the end, but to no avail. I had injected the area with some local anaesthetic, and I remained crouched down by his foot, poking and prodding for a good quarter of an hour. I was struggling, making little progress. The patient, reclining and now almost relaxed on the bed, began to engage me in conversation.

'What do you think about that remarkable young woman who did the operation on the pub floor?' he asked.

What on earth could I say? I felt so embarrassed. In the end I just came clean and told him it was me. He looked me quickly up and down.

'Oh, my goodness. Yes, of course, I recognise you, now. I can't believe you're operating on my foot.' He paused. 'And that you can't seem to do it.'

Two ends of the scale, I appreciated the irony: we both did. Finally I did get the splinter out and he went home happy, saying he was going to tell all his friends that he had a splinter removed from his foot by somebody famous.

There were a few of these lighter moments, but the fall-out from Stephen Niland was a lot to cope with. I was still involved in intensive training and I think my boss, Gareth Davies, was slightly concerned that I'd find it all too overwhelming. He was worried about what I had to learn and that all the media attention might distract me.

With an added dash of humour I tried to carry on regardless of the media and keep things in perspective. I was equally aware that although Alastair had been a big part of it, I was the one receiving the accolade and hype. He just kept on about his business, kept on doing his job. I tried to do the same.

But what had happened on that pub floor in Stratford Broadway had captured the imagination of the media in ways I could never have fathomed. The press would not leave me alone. However wonderful I felt about what we had done on a personal level, I had been publicly lauded: fêted as a heroine, described as 'Heli's Angel' and a miracle worker. The reality was that Friday night in Stratford I was doing my job. Nothing more, nothing less. My job.

12 Flying Solo

I T WAS JUST AFTER MIDDAY ON Bank Holiday Monday, and I was Medic One, in the helicopter on my way to what the call sheet detailed as a fairground accident. My headphones crackled into life.

'Here's some more information for Heather. Someone's fallen and we think they're dead.'

I stared hard at the information sheet I was studying. A young man had fallen from the big wheel. He and his friends had been larking about and showing off, and somehow it had gone too far.

I wasn't looking forward to this one.

This was judgement day, and Gareth Davies was accompanying me in the helicopter. He was about to make up his mind whether or not I was ready to fly as a solo doctor. When you get to the end of your four-week training, as I had now done, Gareth comes out to a few cases to make his final assessment of your on-scene performance. He doesn't do anything other than stand back and watch how you work. He had been out with me a couple of times already, and I had always found it nerve-wracking. So far so good though, but this was the final mission, when he should mark you with his seal of approval – for me it was a rite of passage.

We had the call earlier, and with only the information on the sheet, we had no idea if anyone else was injured or not.

Many thoughts buzzed in my head, as I flicked over to the second page of the call sheet to see which was the nearest hospital.

As we approached the fairground, I could see immediately where the patient lay. All the lights were on, and, as it was a gloomy day, visible from where the helicopter hovered as it prepared to land. Normally the lights of fairs seem bright and cheerful to me but today they were just harsh and garish. There were people all over the fairground – families with young children as well as teenagers – but there was nobody on the north side of the fair where the big wheel stood. Instead, a ring of policemen and fairground officials were keeping people away from the boy. To the side, I could see another, smaller group made up of what I assume were his friends.

The pilot decided to land as near as we could to the scene but we had to be some distance because of the trees surrounding the site of the fair. We landed very gently. A ring of people were watching us, adults and children: this was normal, invariably a crowd of onlookers gathered whenever we showed up in the helicopter. The pilots had to be careful to check that no one was underneath.

Children often get over-excited when we fly in. They run around all over the place, including under the aircraft. Once on Hampstead Heath, just as the helicopter was coming in to land, a dog started barking and ran right underneath us. Fortunately it got blown out of the way, but for a moment my stomach was churning. There are many stories of a landing in Trafalgar Square when a pigeon got caught in the rotor blades. That was enough for me.

Jumping clear of the helicopter we ran the length of the park until we reached the cordon of police officers around the base of the wheel.

Sadly, there was little we could do: we put the boy in the back of the ambulance and took him to hospital. By the time we got there, only a short distance away, it was too late.

For a few minutes afterwards I just sat in the corridor aware of the helplessness creeping up on me. I thought, is that it? Is that all we can do? Yet there was nothing else, nothing for us but to return to the helicopter and fly back to base. The police wanted to talk to us both because there would have to be an inquest. But Gareth told them to come to Whitechapel later in the week to do so. We'd have to write up our notes for them to be of real use in explaining the nature of the fatal injuries for the coroner.

I didn't feel any differently about this case than I do about any of my other patients. At the time, a death, even one as as sad as this, does not overly affect you. This was the only case I had that day, the only opportunity for Gareth to observe me, but I didn't sit and brood. I didn't think any more about it. I spent the rest of my shift doing paperwork and checking out one or two things that had come up as a result of the London Underground training course I'd attended the previous week. It was not until I got home that night that it hit me.

I had worn my flying suit home in the car, and when I got in I didn't take it off immediately. It was, however, warm indoors so I unzipped it to the waist, made myself a cup of tea and slumped on the sofa in front of the television. The news came on, and there was a lot of talk about the fairground accident, accompanied by photographs of the boy who'd died, the fairground itself and, of course, interviews with tearful witnesses. As I sat there absorbed by the coverage of the incident, I looked down and noticed blood on my T-shirt. It must have soaked through my flying suit. It was the boy's blood, and it was his face looking at me from the TV screen. I sat there for a long chilling moment, then I stripped off, went straight into the bathroom and stood under the shower.

Fairgrounds always seem such exciting places, but they're well managed; people do sometimes do silly things they shouldn't, and that's what this boy did, and it killed him. Not only for his friends who were with him but for all those people around who saw it happen, this must have been an awful experience to witness.

I had no further involvement in this case other than to write up my notes for the police and coroner. The police did come by the helipad about a week later to take our statements. On other occasions they'd taken our fingerprints too, which at first I found odd. I always wear my surgical rubber gloves so I had assumed I would leave no fingerprints. But apparently the rubber gloves that we use are so fine you still leave prints behind.

But there was something else too: we video-recorded the call as we often do for training purposes. It is one of the pilots who does the recording and the decision to film the call out had already been made in the helicopter before we knew what or who we were going to find. The pilot on duty went ahead as arranged. Afterwards the police took the tape away as evidence.

This was supposed to be my signing-off case. But it was not appropriate, so officially I was still a trainee. Gareth made this decision because the patient was already clinically dead on our arrival, and apart from an attempt at cardiac massage, there was nothing much I could do for him. I knew I would have to wait a while longer for my first solo flight.

Although the first three weeks of April were among the busiest the HEMS team had ever experienced, there was nothing substantial for me to do for the next few days. In order to sign me off to go solo, Gareth needed to witness me handle one or two reasonable cases. There were calls, but not to anyone who needed very much medical help. There was one to a community college, a child who had fallen backwards off a chair, hit his head on a cupboard and ended up with a little bump on his head. Then I had another patient, a One Under, at one of the tube stations. When I got there I could see from the position of the body that it was impossible for the person to be alive: in fact they'd been run over by the train. This was a pretty unpleasant sight, but what was worse for me was the fact that I could do nothing for them, other than pronounce them life extinct.

Eventually I did have a call where there was activity and an opportunity to do something. This was a 50-foot fall, or a jump. It is invariably a jump, but we call them falls. Fifty feet is considered the cut-off point, a jump from this height is usually fatal, but it can still depend on how and where a person lands, on their age, on whether or not they have taken drugs. Sometimes during the fall they might hit a window ledge or something that slows them down a little. Or they might land on a softer surface such as newly dug earth or grass, which can help prevent fatal injuries. Children tend to survive more often than adults because they are more relaxed and their bones are softer. You can fall from one storey and kill yourself, though you would be unlucky, or you could, with luck, drop fifty feet and survive.

This was a leap from one of London's bridges. Up there you get a view of St Paul's and the city and the busy, often jammed, one-way traffic system that whirls below it.

It is in a very built-up part of London, and unfortunately we had to land quite a long way from the scene and had a long sprint before we could reach the patient. We hitched a ride part way in a passing car: that's always interesting because you have to tell them to drive slowly and carefully, there is no emergency. There you are in your orange suit, your medical pack on your back, having jumped out of a helicopter – of course there's an emergency! But we have to, otherwise members of the general public would be tearing along residential streets, nervous, too fast, thinking they're driving an ambulance. Part of the road there is a one-way system, and we got caught up on the wrong side of it, so our driver could only take us some of the way. We had to run the rest, up hill and with my pack on my back – it was a real struggle.

There was a fair bit of traffic, and the jumper was lying on solid concrete, still alive but only just. They had multiple injuries, literally to every part of the body: head, chest and pelvis, arms and legs. I had to do everything, all the HEMS procedures from start to finish. I started with the neck: collar, airway, breathing, circulation. It becomes very standard, and you become very methodical about it. They had a Glasgow Coma score of three, which meant they were not even responding to pain. It was no surprise that, sadly, they died in hospital three days later.

When I finished that day, Gareth took me into the office and said, 'Well, how do you think it went?' I told him what I thought I could have done better or differently, and when I'd finished, he said, 'Well, I'm happy with you, so that's it. You're free to go.' I was finally signed off.

Now I was scared. I had been desperate to shake off the shackles of training. Now I finally could I was terrified. Up until that point I had always gone out with another doctor. In theory it didn't matter what sort of pickle I might get myself into, not that I ever did in practice, but if I did there was always the comforting knowledge I was not alone. Now I would be alone. It was down to me completely. It was a Friday in early May, and the weekend that followed I flew solo.

The call we received one Saturday morning marked the end of my initiation into HEMS and the start of a new phase. I had arrived early, got all my drugs together and by 8.30 a.m. I was fully prepared to take on the world. Although all the paramedics are excellent, I was blessed to have a particularly experienced one with me that day, Tony Cumner. All the signs were good, and I was raring to go. The first patient had been found by a passer-by on a railway track. It was above ground and we had major problems getting to them. There was nowhere for the helicopter to land, too many cables and power lines. We had to turn the power off to the line and walk a considerable distance before we could attend to the patient. When we arrived they were dead with complete rigor mortis, which sets in about an hour after death, so I did not even try and do anything for them. We had no idea what had happened. There was nothing to indicate that they had been hit by a train, and all we could assume was that, while taking a shortcut home, the patient had tripped over a live rail and been electrocuted.

This was the first case that I had attended on my own. My first solo call and there was nothing we could do. The majority of cases I had seen with HEMS had been multiple trauma, a lot of blood and guts and gore, patients who look a mess. Somehow that makes them less real. This patient looked peaceful, their face perfect and still. I had a gut feeling that this death was no more than a bad decision, a tragic mistake. Most people you find in close proximity to train tracks have tried to commit suicide, so somehow you're less sympathetic, more businesslike about it all. Not so in this case: I had no option but to PLE the patient and walk away.

We left case one at 9.42. It had been an easy one, medically if not psychologically. We got back to the hospital just in time for our next call at 10.24. A small child had fallen from the top of a flight of stairs. We got to the scene at 10.40, where we found the child upset and crying, but nevertheless alert and orientated, which is medical speak for awake and talkative. She had been climbing up the outside of the stairs and fallen about 15 feet, slapping her head on the stone floor when she landed. She was with a babysitter – an auntie or some other close relative – who was extremely distraught. One of the ambulance paramedics comforted her, while I concentrated on the little girl.

She had not been knocked out by the fall, and the only external injury appeared to be a bit of a swelling on her head, though she was bleeding a little from her ears and nose. Essentially, there was little wrong with her that I could see, but I decided that because she had fallen so far, the chances of internal injury were quite high, so I sent her to the nearest neurological centre, which was at the local hospital. We took her by ambulance, leaving the scene at eleven o'clock. As I had first surmised, her injuries did not turn out to be significant, probably to do with 'floppy-child syndrome' – they're far more relaxed fallers.

I was wary of calls to children. I'd attended one in my first week with Alastair. This was to a very young child who had fallen backwards off a playground step. I'd been the observer up until then – this was the first time I was Medic One. When we were in the helicopter going out, I said to Alastair, 'I just hope it's not a child.' The sheet came over my shoulder, and what was it? A three-year-old. I completely froze. I just sat there thinking I can't do this. I really can't do this.

If you know the child's age, you can start calculating all the different things you need to know for each age group such as what tube you might need to use if you have to intubate and what doses of the drug you are going to give. You can work everything out in advance. But on that occasion I couldn't. My brain had ground to a halt. I told Alastair as much.

'Yes you can. Come on. Write this down. Good, that's it. Now this.' He prodded me verbally, reassuringly.

I was nervous about children, because I know they are so much more complicated and I have much less experience of them. There is more to think about because of the age and weight differentials. Also they can't tell you as much and they can deteriorate a lot faster. You have got to be very careful with them.

Around about 16, in fact from puberty onwards, people become more standard, although men and women are different, of course. The tube with which we intubate people is a length and a diameter, and when you go to intubate someone you take out the one that you think will be right for them, as well as one bigger and one smaller. The rule of thumb is nine for a man, and eight for a woman, plus or minus a little either way. Often with children you can look at how big their nose is or their little finger – that gives you some indication of what size tube you need to use. As for drugs, I can guess people's weights very easily now, so I know vaguely what I need to give and I can adjust it accordingly.

In the end the child turned out to have done himself no harm and did not need any medical intervention at all, but for those few seconds in the helicopter I was in a blind panic.

Back at the helipad later, I devised a chart that fitted into the flight book that lived in my pocket. On it I tabulated all the drug doses and equipment sizes I would require for children of different ages and body weight. So, no matter if I was in a complete panic, I could just refer to the chart and I wouldn't make a mistake.

That first weekend solo I did not get one moment's peace. We arrived at the hospital at 11.15 with the little girl. It took us about half an hour to get things sorted out there, and we had just taken off for our helipad when we got the next call. It had come in to London Ambulance Control at 12.02 and got to us by 12.15. Another child: for someone who was apprehensive about treating them, I was surely tested that day.

In the grounds of the housing estate where he lived, we found a young boy who had fallen off a climbing frame, a distance of about five feet. When we arrived on scene he was actually on his back with his legs still stuck in the frame, and everybody was too scared to move him. His parents, his brothers and sisters, were all running around in a state of shock, and I had to try and keep them away from him while I worked out what to do. He was all twisted up with his neck and his back shunted round, and he lay at the base of the frame, his body at an awkward angle. He was complaining of pain in his ankle, but that was all. When I asked him if he had any pain in his neck, he told me he didn't. It seemed an improbable answer, because it looked so contorted, but when I asked him if he could straighten it he did so without any problem at all. After that we just lifted him out. He was fine. At first glance it looked as though he had broken his neck in half, but in fact, he'd only sprained an ankle.

We left the scene at 12.41, and we got back to the London around 13.00. All we ever eat up on the helipad is toasted sandwiches, because it is the only food that gets provided. We used to melt the cheese in the microwave and spread it on toast. I had made one for my lunch but hadn't got it anywhere near my mouth when the next call came in. 13.19. I could not believe my continuing bad luck. But on this occasion the call was to a baby not a child, a very young baby and a sick one at that.

When we arrived on scene, the ambulance crew told us it was upstairs in a flat on the seventh floor. There had been a domestic accident and the baby had been laid out on the floor, where the ambulance men had started to do some basic life support. My first thought was the baby was tiny, and I tried to work out what size tubes to use. It was right off the scale of my chart. Adult tubes have a diameter the size of a penny piece, but this one was no bigger than a child's drinking straw: I had to get it in to ventilate the lungs. It went in on my first attempt. I got one of the paramedics to start CPR. To perform cardiac compressions on a baby you put your hands round the entire chest and start squeezing in a pincer movement. Once we had started doing that, I looked to see what the injuries were. There was a huge swelling round the back of the head, which was not a good sign. I had no real idea at this stage whether this tiny tot stood a chance at all. It was clear the injuries were bad, very bad, but babies can survive the most surprising things.

With the CPR going, we performed what we call 'Scoop and Run' to get the infant to hospital and more facilities. I carried it out of the room and down the stairs. I had to walk past the mother, and I could not bring myself to look at her because I was on the verge of tears myself and her stricken face would have tipped me over the edge. I was really struggling with my emotions now: this was my third child of the day. We got the baby into the ambulance and took it to the local hospital. The staff who received me were extremely nice. They must have realised how upset I was and they took over immediately. I was no longer part of it. I had done all that I could and I went to sit outside and drink a cup of tea with the ambulance crew. I found out later that at one point the baby got a heart output back, but that did not last. Its pulse flickered briefly and then was gone entirely.

Someone came out afterwards to have a word with me. 'You did a really good job. There was nothing more you could have done.'

I was devastated, such a tiny child, such a terribly tragic waste.

One of the things you do after someone you've treated dies is rack your brains – you literally agonise over it. Was there something else I could have done that might have saved them? What if I'd done this? What if I'd done that? Would it have made any difference? Could I have done something better?

This was my worst case ever, and one that will stay with me for the rest of my life.

Our next call was just outside London to a caravan park. The helicopter was actually able to land within the park, so we were close to where we needed to be and quickly on scene. We found a man, about fifty, who had fallen from the roof on to his back.

He was really combative, fighting us, kicking at us – all the signs of a bad head injury. So I put him to sleep and then did bilateral thoracostomies. Because I knew that his injuries were really severe, I flew him back to the London. The trauma team found severe brain swelling, a fractured neck and chest injuries. He died the next day.

So, that day was not a good day for me. And it hadn't finished yet. Our final call that night was at 19.01, which we just fitted in before the helicopter went home to comply with the darkness curfew. We landed in the heart of central London, just behind the John Lewis department store. Another tourist had been hit by a bus on Oxford Street, probably looking the wrong way when crossing the road. The patient had actually been knocked out for a few minutes, and kept asking what had happened, over and over again. The problem with non-English speakers is that you're not able to decide for sure if they are confused just because of the language and difficulty communicating, or because of a head injury. Mercifully, there was nothing seriously wrong with the patient who, having been taken to a nearby hospital, was later checked out and discharged.

We had responded to six calls that day. I went home, but I had no time to recover. There was no possibility of being broken in gently. I ate, went to sleep and woke up again. Then I was back at the helipad and attending the second most awful case I experienced with HEMS. This was yet another child of about ten or twelve years old. A bus had reversed over the child, the driver having not seen him because he was so short. He was completely trapped under the rear nearside wheel. The ambulance service got the call at eleven o'clock on the Sunday morning, and we were on scene six minutes later.

He was still stuck under the bus, and had been for a quarter of an hour. He had lost his output and with no pulse he was effectively dead. Tony and I clambered underneath the vehicle. Lying there on the road with the weight of the lorry on top of us we tried to perform cardiac compressions, and intubate and ventilate him. We needed to give him intravenous adrenaline to help get his heart going, but there was nowhere to put a line. I could not lift my head more than an inch. It was dark, pitch black and dirty. It was impossible to get a line in. I tried both arms, his groin: desperately I made cuts on his ankles, sometimes you can see the vein and put a line in there. I failed. I tried his neck and I failed again. I could find nowhere to set up a drip.

The other problem was that he had a hugely inflated thorax, trapped air in one side of his chest and the other side deflated. So I made a hole in the inflated side and released the air. It didn't do him any good. He had massive internal injuries. It was too late to call the Fire Brigade. Usually they were there by the time we arrived on scene, activated by the ambulance crew or the police, or sometimes I would call them out. This time there was no point, any work that could be done had to be done while he lay where he was. By the time they had been able to move the vehicle off him it would have been too late to do anything anyway.

Vividly I remember something that haunts me, and I think it always will: a pool of sludge-like green goo that surrounded this child as he lay trapped under that bus. It took me a while to work out what it was. He must have been helping his mother with the shopping when the vehicle hit him: a bottle of Fairy Liquid had burst, the contents leaking out to encircle him like green blood. It was so simple, so very tragic, like the man on the railway line yesterday. I tried and tried: I was Medic One and I wasn't just going to quit. But I could not get a pulse back. In the end something clicked in my head, some safety valve maybe. I looked one last time at Tony, my paramedic, then certified him dead, as we lay under the bus.

I felt so guilty afterwards, as if I had not done my best. I think it was because I'd failed to get a line into him to give him any drugs or fluids. But I simply could not manage it, nobody could. I knew it deep down, but the despair was the same as the baby yesterday, two in two days. Again I racked my brains thinking if there was anything I could have tried, any other way of getting that line in. I don't actually think it would have made any difference, but I wish now that I'd just pulled him out from underneath the bus, regardless of whether or not it might have exacerbated certain injuries. I would have had the advantage of more room to manoeuvre, possibly more options if he'd been on the side of the road. But he was dead anyway: he had no pulse, he couldn't get any worse. I was chastising myself again, forgetting right then that there's nothing as wise as hindsight.

God only knows what the driver was going through. It had been an accident, he could not have been blamed, but he would serve a life sentence mentally anyway – not a single day would go by without him thinking of ways he could have avoided that child. We don't often see the drivers. The police take them away and sit them in a car or give them a cup of tea. They always get taken to hospital for a check-up, but there is not much anyone can do except make sure they have someone to talk to. Obviously they are in shock. This was death number four this weekend, and I was beginning to wonder why. This was my first solo weekend and I felt awful. Maybe I'd been spoiled, spared some of the reality after the incredible high I'd experienced after Stephen Niland had lived against such unlikely odds.

Life went on though, my shift went on. At 14.30 we were out again. Yet another tourist, no bus this time, and not Oxford Street, but west: a woman had fallen down the escalater at one of the central London tube stations and whacked the back of her head. When we got there she was going completely berserk. It was the same story: I couldn't decide whether this was the result of a head injury or her inability to communicate. Eventually someone was able to translate for us. We found out that she was due to catch a flight in two hours. We had been cutting off her clothes to examine her, and she was furious with us. She was adamant that she would not miss her flight, and I was equally insistent she should not fly until she had been thoroughly examined at the nearest hospital. As it turned out there was no real damage, but they kept her in for 24 hours' observation. She missed her plane and we'd ruined her clothes, and she was fuming about it. Sometimes patients are not as grateful as they might be!

Same day we got called to a casino, where a woman had been assaulted. I shall always remember landing at this major crossroads. The awning of a nearby florist was torn by the huge downdraught from the helicopter and left shredded and flapping in the breeze. Every plant, every flower on display on the pavement was blown over and ruined: the whole shop was left in an unsightly mess, though amazingly the florist herself was very nice about it.

If that was a mess, what we found on scene was a battlefield by comparison. The patient had been shot in the chest and abdomen. She didn't have a pulse, and multiple wounds punctured her body. She was wearing heavy make-up and glamorous clothes, and the scene looked like something out of a bad horror movie.

I had an observer with me, a journalist who had arrived at lunch time. He had been queasy in the helicopter and was definitely looking greener now.

I performed a thoracotomy on the patient to try and get her pulse back, but her chest was full of blood. A bullet had gone through a major blood vessel that could not be repaired. There was nothing more I could do. Immediately I signed her as dead on scene.

So that was my first weekend: two silly accidents, a faller and the poor baby. Now here was yet another life totally laid wasted. My first weekend. We got back to Whitechapel at about 17.30, where we had to stay until 19.00 in case we had another call. I felt as depressed as I ever have done. Five PLEs in two days: heavy stuff for anyone. I had seen the odd person die during the previous month, but never such a catalogue as this. I began to feel uneasy and paranoid. Why now, the first time I was on my own? Why were all my patients dying? Was it me, the so-called 'Heli's Angel'? Was I losing my touch?

13 The Last Tango

I F YOU CAN'T STAND THE HEAT, GET OUT of the kitchen: HEMS is traumatic for everyone. If you are not able to cope with it, then you should not be doing it. It's as simple as that. At the weekly Death and Doughnuts meeting, I was able to talk through my weekend from hell with the others. It helped immensely. People always ask me whether we had counselling at HEMS. No, we didn't. But we were friends, all part of the same tight-knit group. We counselled each other, and that included the fire crew and the pilots. We really are one big team and, when I got back to base between calls that weekend, the fire crew were always willing and ready to make me a cup of tea. Later, the other doctors would ask after me, making sure I was OK, wanting to know what had happened on my shifts, particularly given it was my first time solo. That was all it took, the support of my colleagues. Tea and sympathy was the best prescription for me.

Even though it is not officially classified as counselling, this level of support from colleagues is very important. We do the same job. They know what it's like and how it feels. Although each case is different, there are similarities, and there will always be someone who's had a similar experience to you. The doctors who were there when I was were superb. The whole team was fantastic. That's what I miss most about it, really. It was family life at its best.

The teamwork and support that you get at HEMS is unique in the medical profession. Of course other hospital teams are supportive of one another, but not to the same degree. Tending to patients on the street heightens the drama, tension and involvement of the job. It is all very instant. You can save and lose people on the spot, literally in a heartbeat. This is the front line: you see so much trauma, so much life and death, blood and gore and guts, the bonding is that much stronger. A&E departments depend on huge teamwork, but a hospital unit is team playing on a large scale, and I never found that I got as close to people there as I did working on HEMS.

It is never possible to become indifferent to death or injuries. When you lose people, as I had done that first weekend, you start to question yourself, your professional ability and wonder whether you're doing something wrong. That is a natural and human response. The job requires us to develop a particularly thick skin, but not so thick we become arrogant. When you have doubts like mine, the team are there to support you, sensitively but not blindly. If there was something I did wrong or could have done better I wanted to know about it. We all would. I was really pleased to come to work on the Monday and discuss it with Gareth and the others.

Death and Doughnuts has evolved into a staple of the HEMS diet, both a blowhole and a discussion platform to enable us to cope with the job and learn to do it better. It is a variable session in terms of timing, depending on when we're all around and when Gareth can fit it in. Doughnuts are slang for the CT scanners, the big hollow circle that patients go through, but it is also a reference to the tradition, now lapsed, of having a cake with our coffee during the debriefing.

It is a bit like confession time: you always feel better afterwards, just talking things through is incredible therapy. It helps you to focus on the positive as well as the negative, enables you deal more easily with frayed emotions. It allows you to discover your weaknesses and there's advice from good people if there's room for improvement. No one is perfect – we're as human and fragile as the people we are called to assist.

By the end of my session that Monday I genuinely believed there was nothing else I could have done for any of the patients who had died on me over the weekend. That eased the weight immeasurably, it was vital if I was going to go on.

Gareth Davies was great, and he put it very succinctly when he said: 'Listen, this is HEMS. You had an almost unfortunate start, because you had nice things happen to you. You had survivors who should never have survived. But this is the reality of it. People die, and we see lots of deaths. It will balance itself out. You'll find that from next week you won't have any. Then you'll get another spate again.'

He was right, of course. It did me a lot of good and I learned to cope – and quickly. I realised that sometimes you needed the hide of a rhinoceros, that good and bad are integral parts of the same continuum. I had got off lightly at first, and now fate had clamped down hard on me to redress the balance. What I needed and what I ultimately achieved was the ability to switch off, leave HEMS where it belonged on that darkened helipad when the shift was over.

Dancing is perfect for this, a focus that is vibrant and energetic and full of life. It's a marvellous contrast, a foil for what I do in the daytime. Plus the exercise is wonderfully relaxing after a hard day's doctoring. I have been dancing for five years now as a principal with the London Theatre of Ballroom at Claridge's and the Hippodrome, at Madame Jo-Jo's and Whitehall Palace. I do about two shows a month, which I fit in around work. I received an invitation to appear on the Esther Rantzen show to talk about this very topic: professionals who lead a double life.

Just before I joined HEMS. I was working in A&E at the Charing Cross Hospital and dancing on Sundays at the Café de Paris. One moment I would be dealing with a man who was seriously injured after falling down a lift shaft, wearing my white coat and a stethoscope round my neck; the next I was performing before a room full of people attending a tea dance.

I used to split my shift where the hospital would allow me. I'd go to work dressed in theatre greens and trainers. I would leave halfway through to do the afternoon show, then return to A&E in full stage make-up the same evening.

On another occasion I did an advert for Heinz foods. It was to promote one of their Mediterranean Meals, and I went to the Rivoli in Brockley for filming. It was a day's work, but I earned as much in 12 hours as a doctor does in 120. I had to dance the Argentine tango, the slinkiest and most intimate version of the dance, dressed in huge red sequins that made skimpy and low cut look overdressed. My nails were fitted with acrylic extensions and my hair dyed jet black. Even my neighbour, who has lived below me for the past ten years, failed to recognise me when I returned home that night and passed him in the hallway. I was back working at the Chelsea and Westminster the next day though, the nails soaked off in acetate, the hair almost back to its usual browny blonde.

A sense of humour helps, and sometimes even a HEMS call gave us the chance to have a laugh. There was a touch of black humour to a case that we went to in Stratford High Street – a pedestrian had been hit by a hearse, which still had the body on board, lying in the back in its coffin. The patient had had a couple of drinks, and had presumably walked across the road in front of the hearse. The accident resulted in a fractured arm and neck, and a minor head injury. He was hospitalised, but made good progress and finally went home in one piece.

On another occasion when I was Medic One, with Sean as my paramedic, we were called to assist a guy who had fallen and hit his pelvis while trying to climb over the balcony of his flat. I think he was play-acting a little, the helicopter had come out to him, and he was suddenly the focus of attention, surrounded by all of his mates. He was moaning and whinging so much he would have looked good on a continental football pitch. If he had been seriously hurt, there would have been none of that because the shock would take over.

It was the hottest day of the year, the middle of June, a real scorcher. By nine in the morning I was already feeling the heat in my flying suit and perspiring quietly. I don't sweat a great deal and nothing compared to Sean. No one sweats as much as Sean. It fairly runs off his head, like a tap you can't quite turn off.

This patient was lying on the ground, moaning, his eyes closed, and Sean was leaning over him trying to put on a pelvic splint. As he was working droplets of his sweat were dripping on the patient's trousers. All at once in his weak and pathetic voice he began to apologise, 'Oh, God. I'm really sorry, I've wet myself.'

He hadn't. Sean had perspired all over him. I suppose we could have put him straight, but we didn't. We left him to stew, cheeks flushed with embarrassment, a great patch of damp across his groin. We took him to hospital, where, not surprisingly, he was discharged the same day.

One summer day, I was pulling a patient out of the River Thames. He was soaking wet and struggling as he didn't want to go in the ambulance. I was up to my waist in filthy water and river mud when my mobile phone rang.

'It's Richard Branson calling from Necker.'

I couldn't respond except to start laughing.

He said, 'Is this a bad time?'

'Well, yes, I suppose so,' I replied.

'I just wanted to ask if you'd consider writing your story for Virgin. Please call me back when you've got a minute.'

So *that*'s how this book came about.

We do follow the progress of our patients and I always tried to phone the day after we got them to hospital. If they were seriously ill I would monitor progress by calling at weekly intervals. If I had a really busy week then it sometimes might be a couple before I got the chance to make the phone call. It takes for ever: you have to go through the switchboard, then find what ward the patient is on. Obviously the nurses will not give out information to just anyone, so you have to prove who you are, and quite often they refuse to tell you anything unless they phone you back to check that you are really who you say you are. It can take up to half an hour per patient. Sometimes they've already been discharged, so they have to fish out the files.

Once they are discharged I mark the top of the sheet with a red biro. This was something I did off my own back, and not a requirement of the job.

I care what happens to my patients. But, in this job you have to remember that not even your best can help all the time. As Gareth Davies says, we look death in the face every day of our lives.

When I was out with George one day during my training month, we were called to a shooting just as the helicopter was leaving for the night. It was dusk, but not yet dark, and the pilots decided there was still time to take us. The patient had been shot in the street and still had a pulse when we got there, but lost it in A&E before we left. There was nobody in the trauma team capable of doing a thoracotomy so George and I performed one in the department. The trauma team were happy for us to do so, and we did everything we could, but sadly the patient died. When the patient was opened up, we discovered massive internal injuries.

The helicopter should have flown back to Denham after it had dropped us at the scene of the stabbing, but that day they waited for us and flew us back to Whitechapel. To go back on the tube to the Royal London at that time of night in our bloodied orange flying suits was a prospect we hardly relished, so we were delighted. By the time we were ready to leave it was dark. The helicopter should have been back in its hangar by now but the pilots had kindly waited. As we flew over London I couldn't help but appreciate just how beautiful it looked. We passed Tower Bridge, its illuminated structure mingling with the streetlights like strings of pearls glittering over the city. The contrast between this ordered panorama of light, pulsing now with night-life and the grim chaos of the Casualty department, was enormous. One minute we were elbow-deep in blood as death claimed its own, the next we're looking down on this. Twin aspects of life in this city: the ugliness and beauty in the same split moment.

The helicopter dropped us at the helipad and then flew straight to Denham. It was early evening now, around 19.00, maybe. At 19.15, Alastair, who had now finished his HEMS tour of duty, dropped by to visit me. Everyone else had gone home, and we sat in the doctors' Portakabin by the helipad, chatting amiably over a cup of coffee. The phone rang at 19.30. Unbelievably it was Aubrey, the paramedic who had phoned from Central Ambulance Control on the night Stephen Niland was stabbed.

'Just wanted to see if any of you were there,' he said. 'Heather, you're not going to believe this. There's been a stabbing. Can you respond?'

I looked at Alastair. I could hardly bring myself to speak. *Déjà vu*: exactly the same time of night, the same person phoning, and the two of us on the helipad.

But we could not attend in the Audi. Alastair was on call for Anaesthetics, and he was not able to leave the hospital, and I am not trained to drive the car with lights and sirens. So I told Aubrey I was quite happy to go but Alastair could not come with me. Could he arrange for a vehicle to come and get me?

'Yup,' he said, 'I'll get back to you. Get your gear together and go and wait by the entrance. I'll send an ambulance to collect you.'

So I waited, but by the time they managed to get somebody to pick me up the patient had already been scooped up by another ambulance. It was taking too long to get me there and they could not risk waiting. They took him to casualty. Like Stephen Niland, the patient possibly needed a thoracotomy, but he didn't get one. He was dead when he got to hospital.

I left HEMS after six months, took my Greek holiday and started my MSc in Sports Medicine. It is a perfect combination for me, bringing together my twin passions of medicine and dance. One day, who knows, I might be doctor to a premiership football team, something currently out of bounds to women. But 'out of bounds' has always been my speciality. I am no abider of limits. I have had a few close shaves along the way, but I would never have it otherwise. My life is exciting, which is the way I want it. At last with my MSc I'm able to reconcile my love of dancing with my passion for medicine. I love them both equally: one could not fully exist without its alter ego. Given all that I've told you, you might suppose I've become hardened to death, to serious injury. But I haven't. I will never be blasé about death and I will never forget just how privileged you feel if you get to save a life.